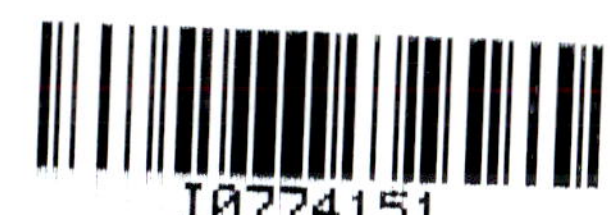

THIS BOOK BELONGS TO

To Access Other
GOLDMINE
SCAN THE QR CODE
AND UNLOCK

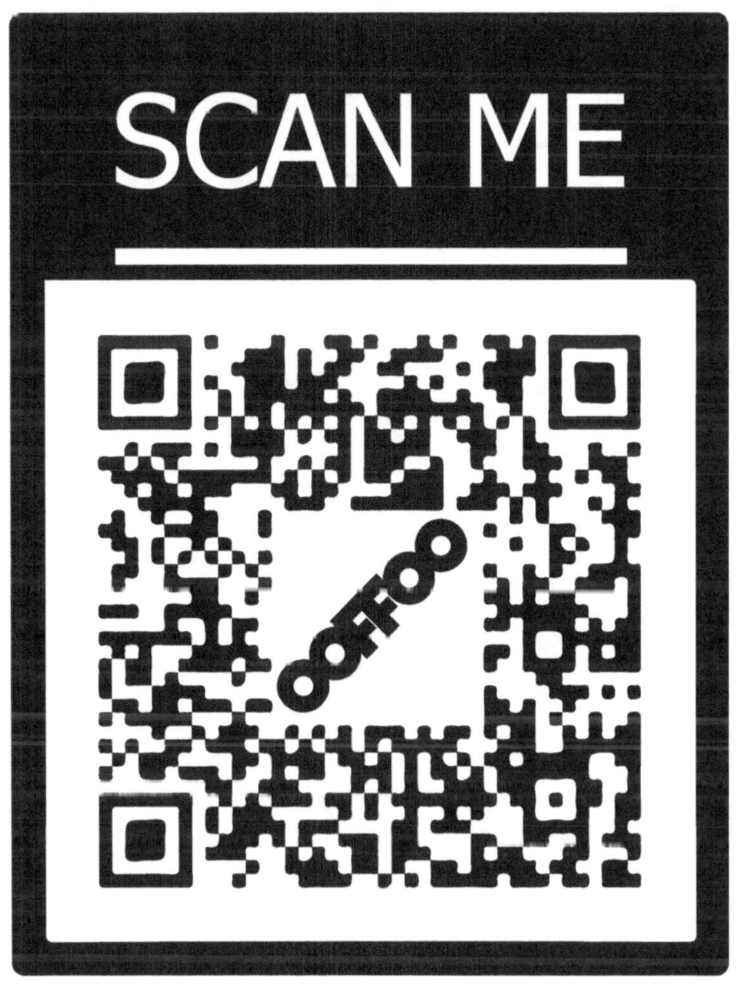

Test Your Color Here

Test Your Color Here

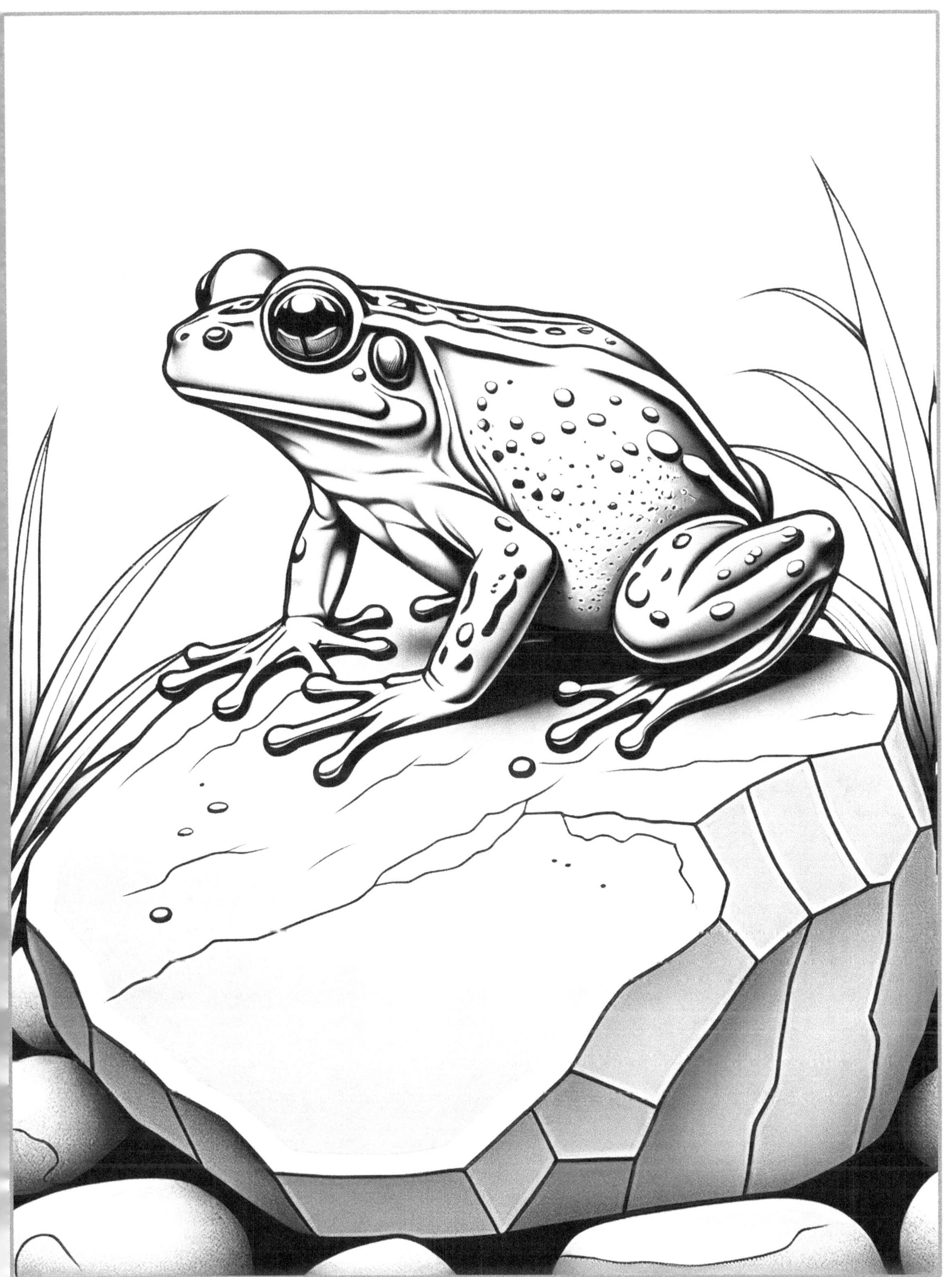

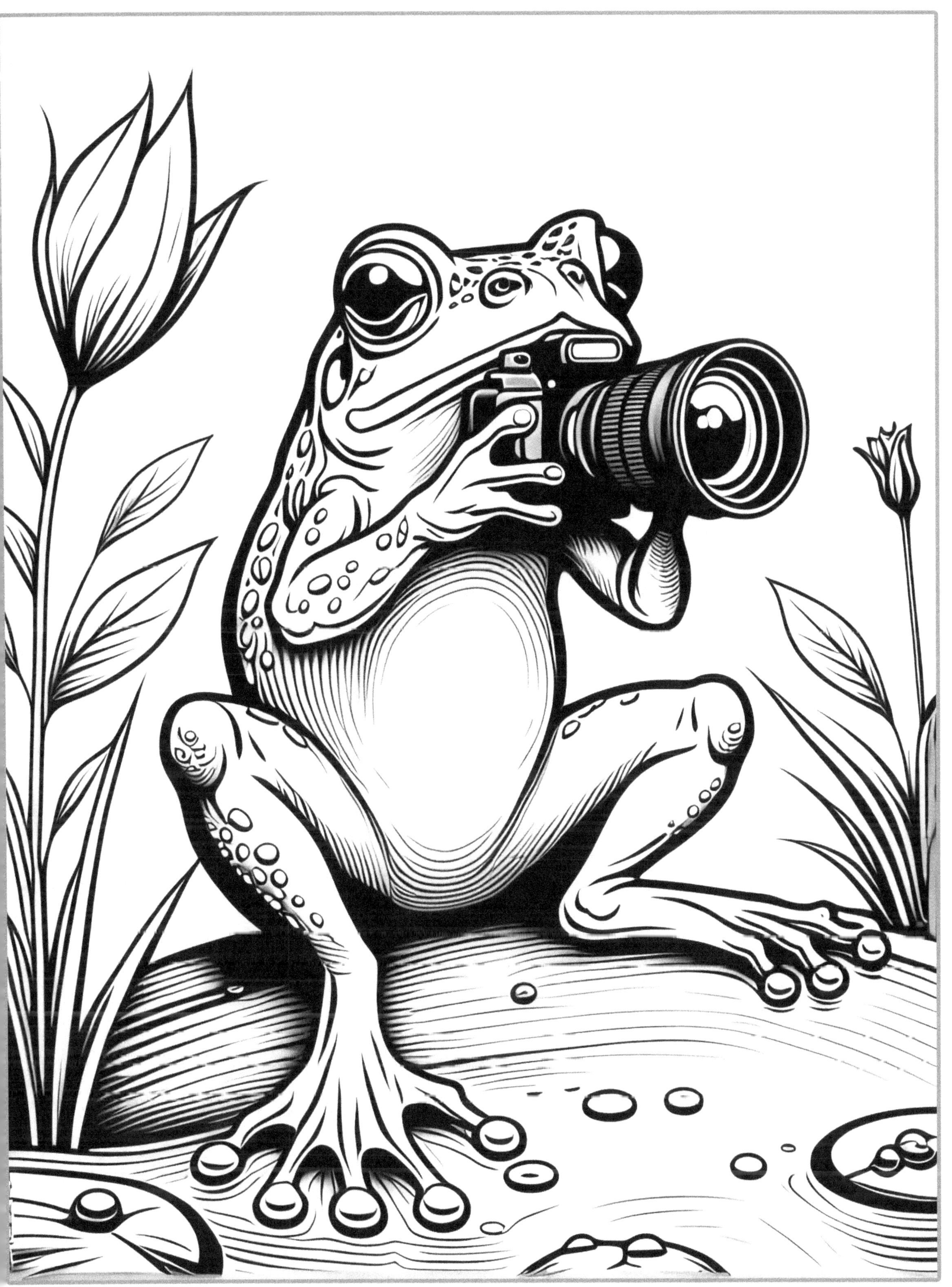

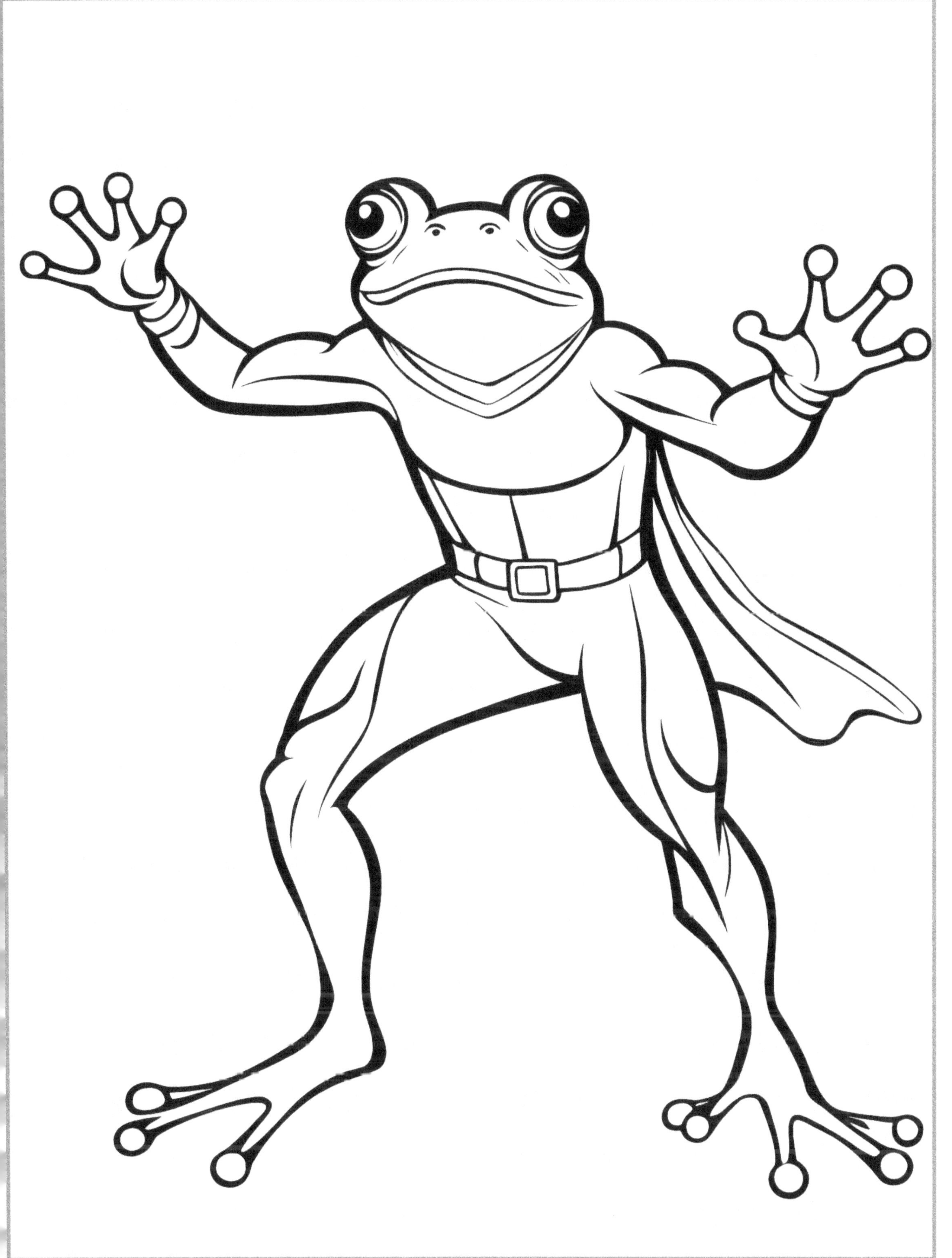

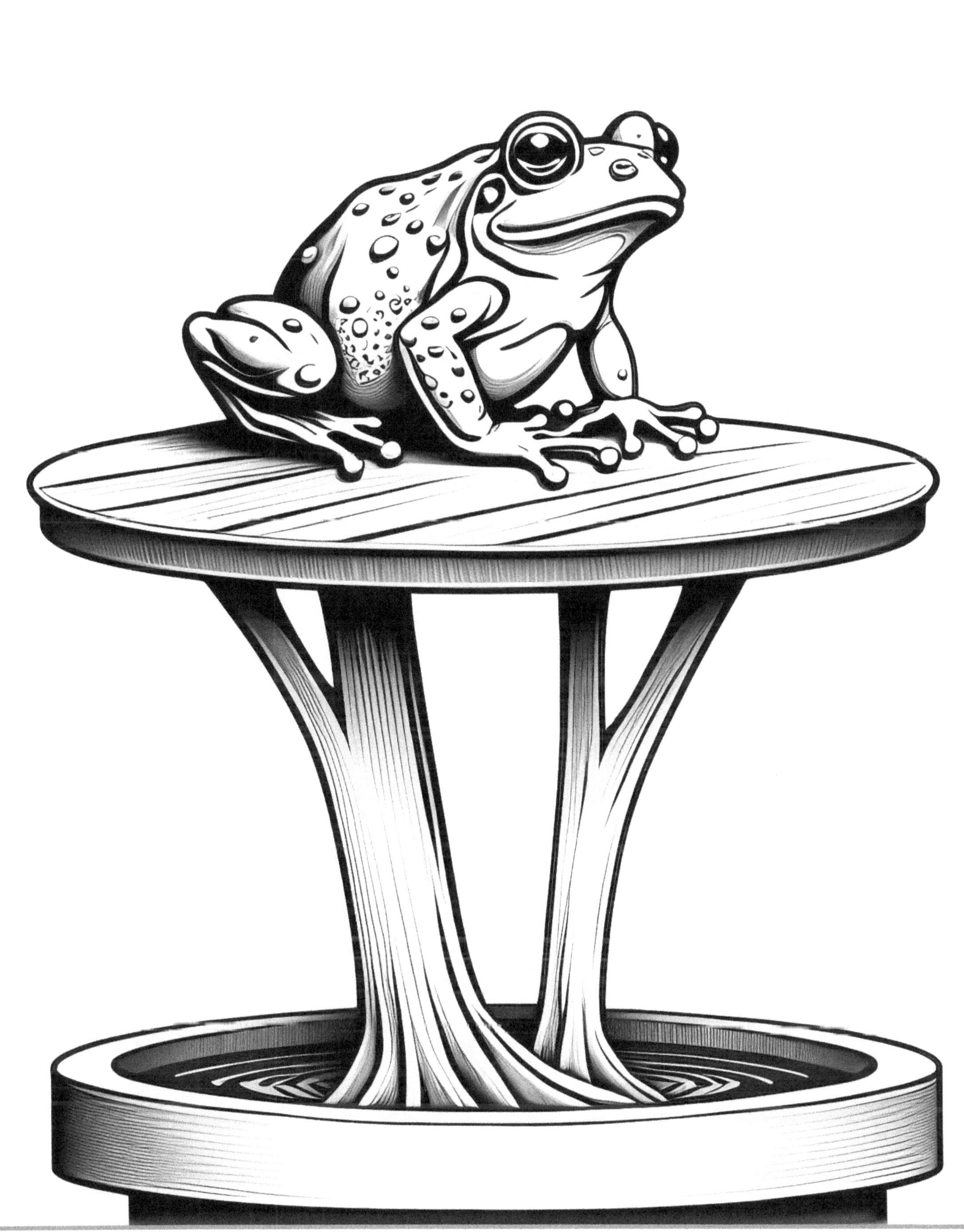

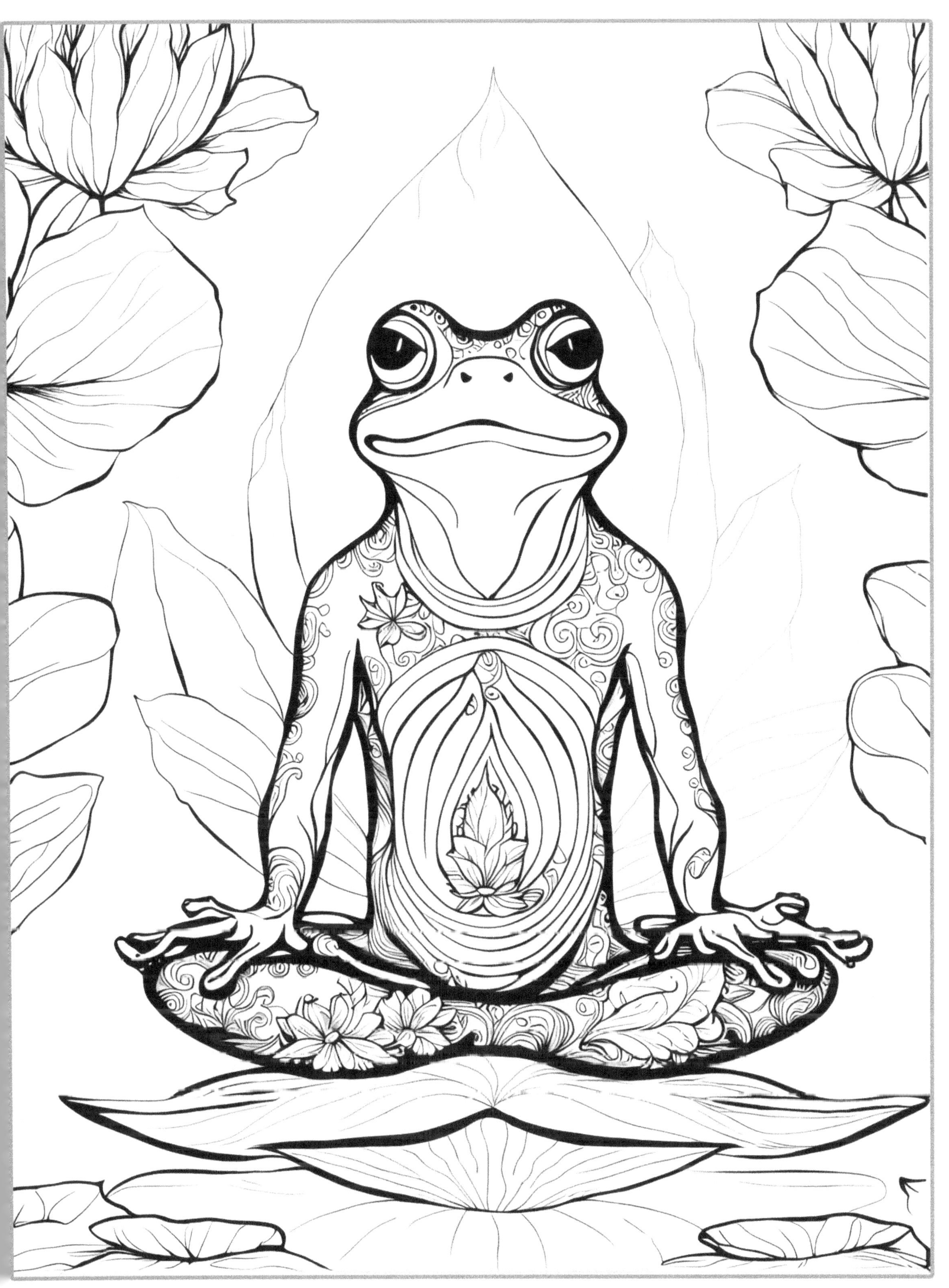

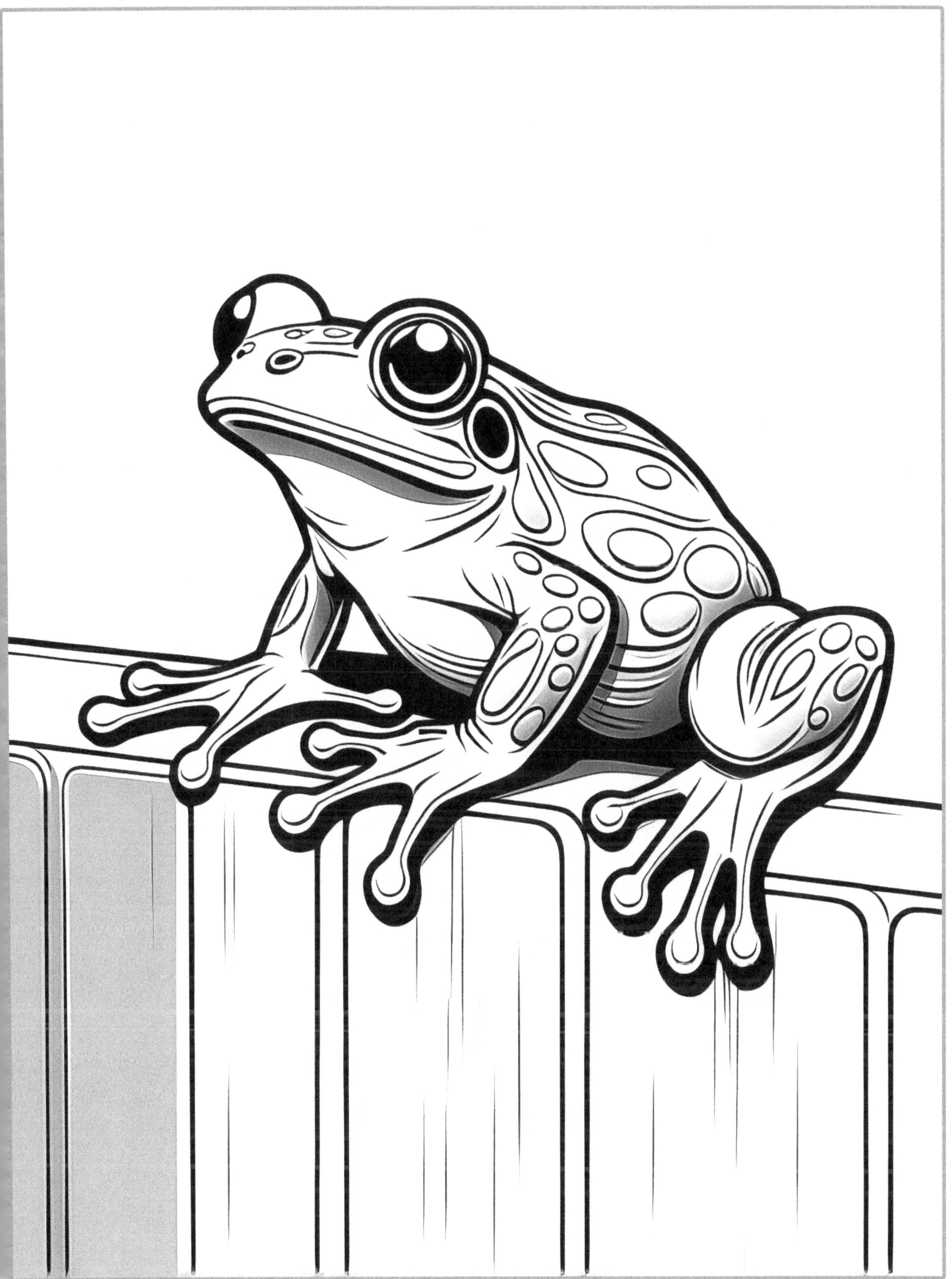

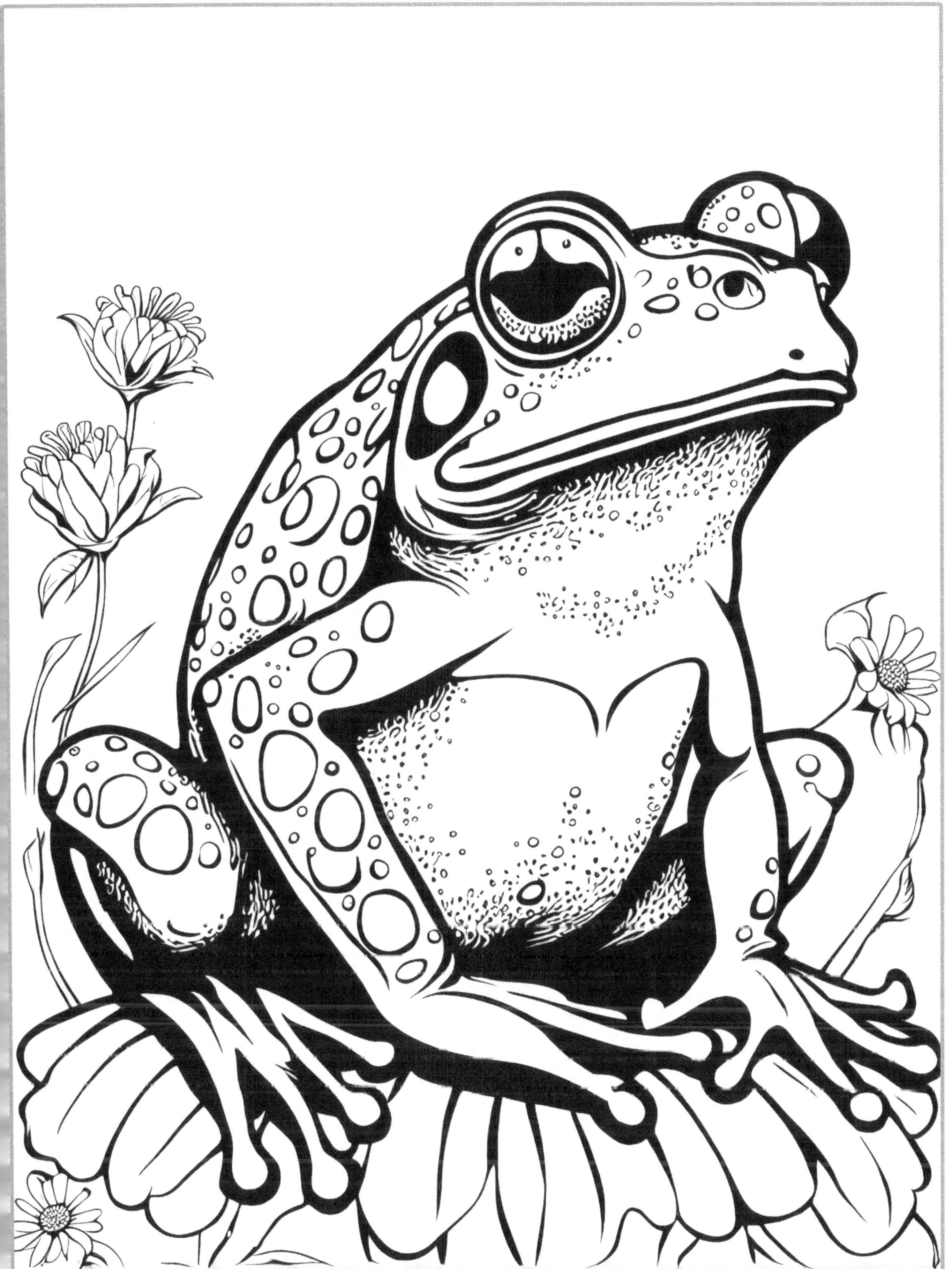

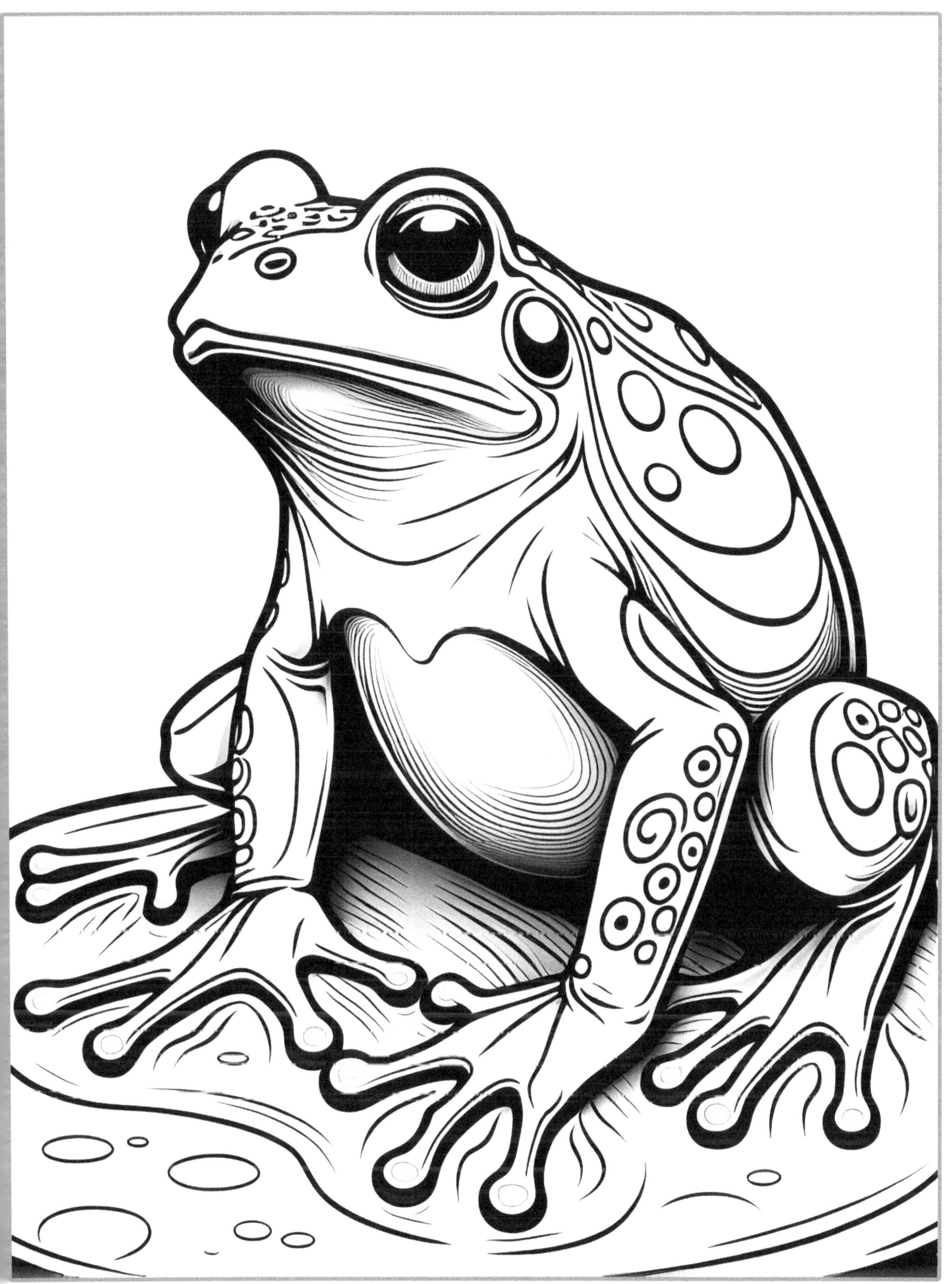

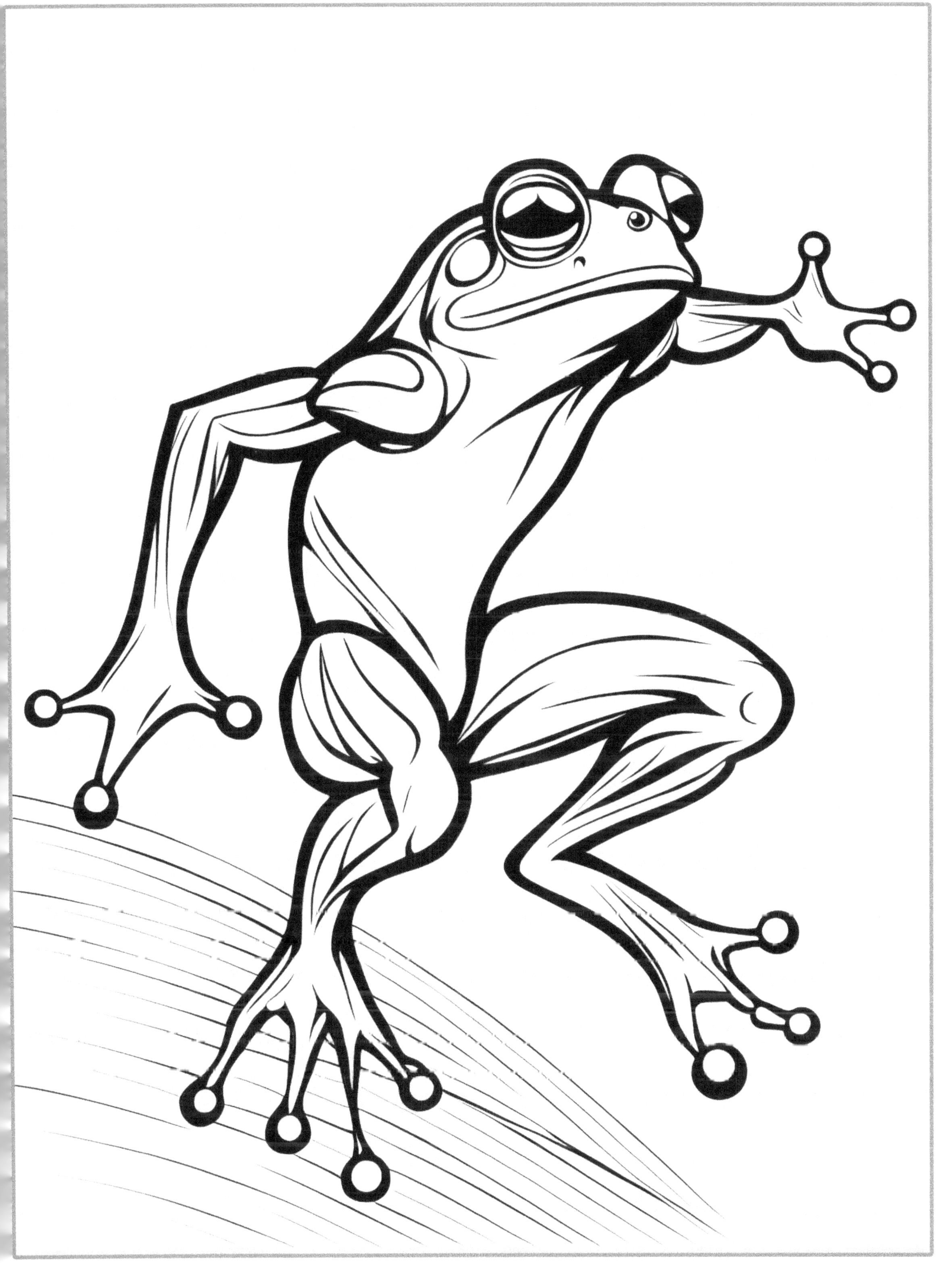

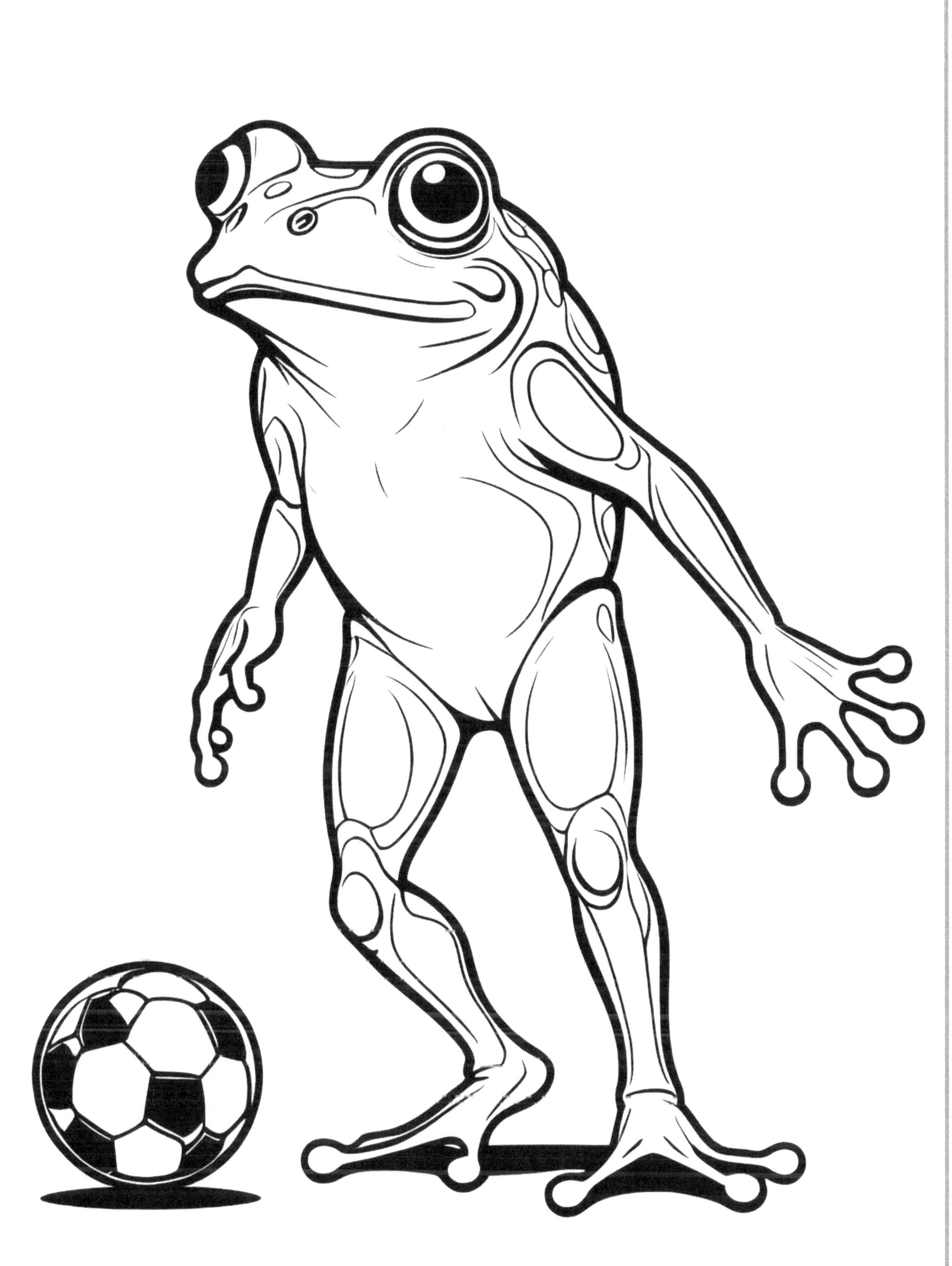

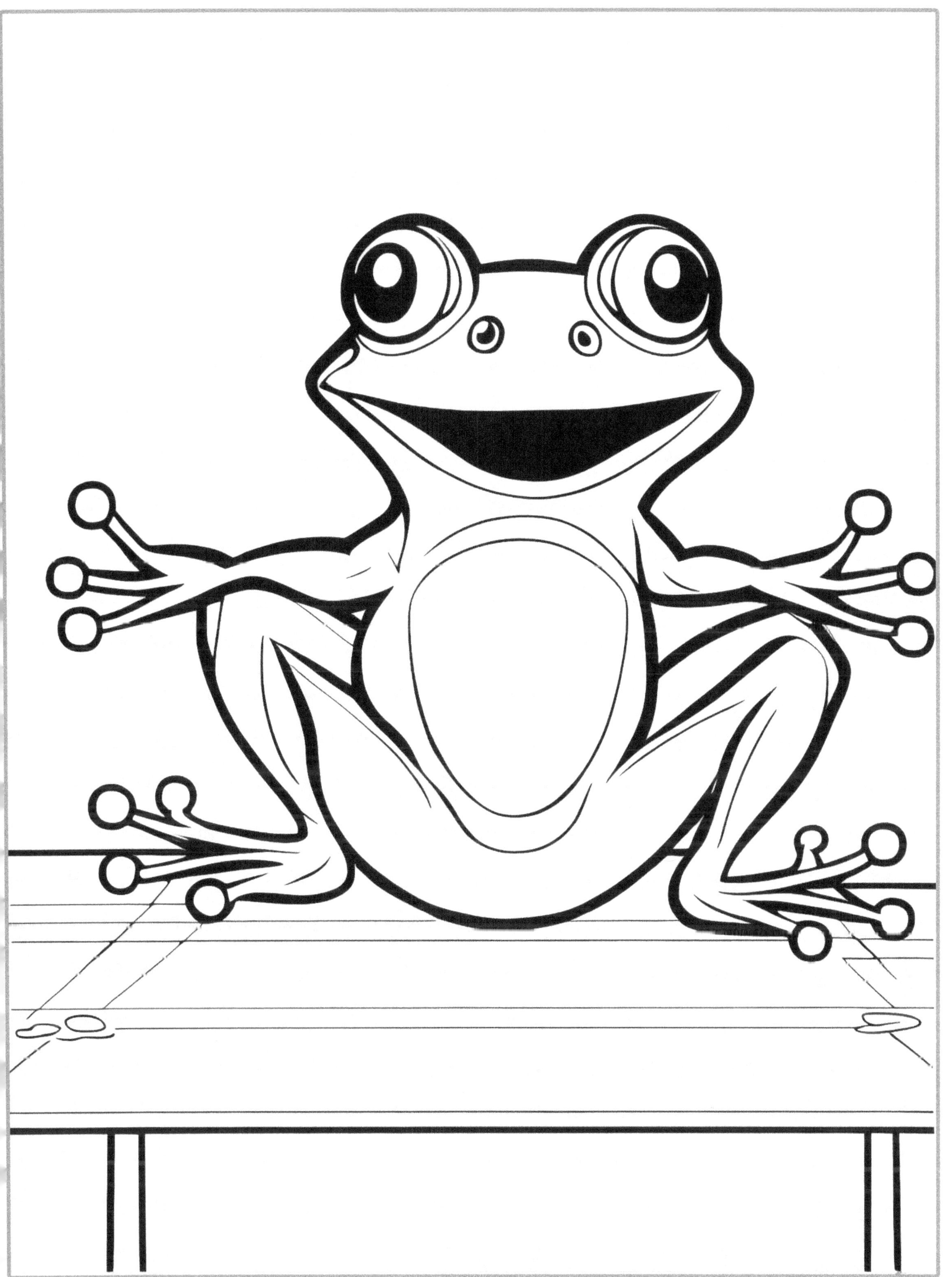

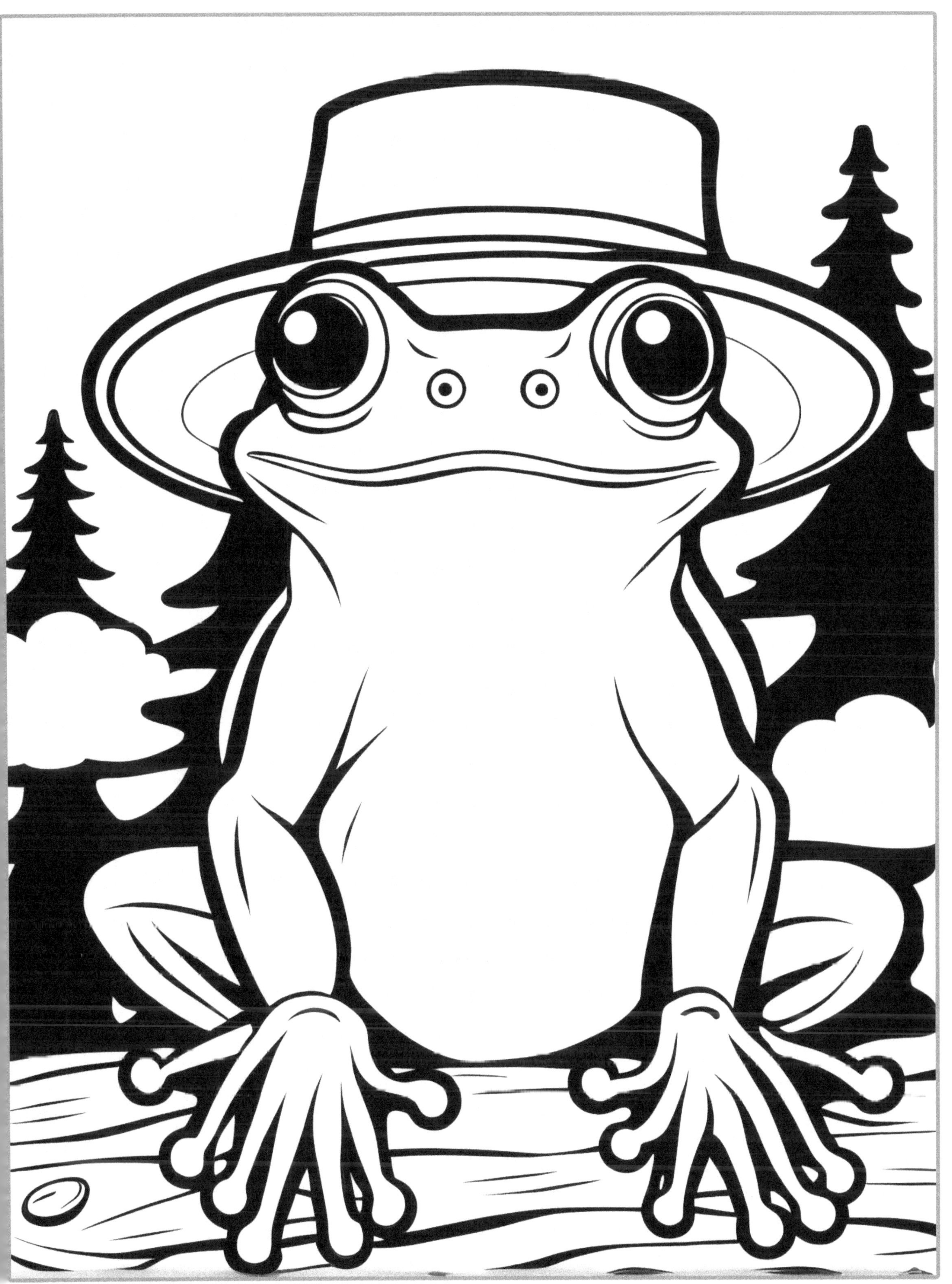

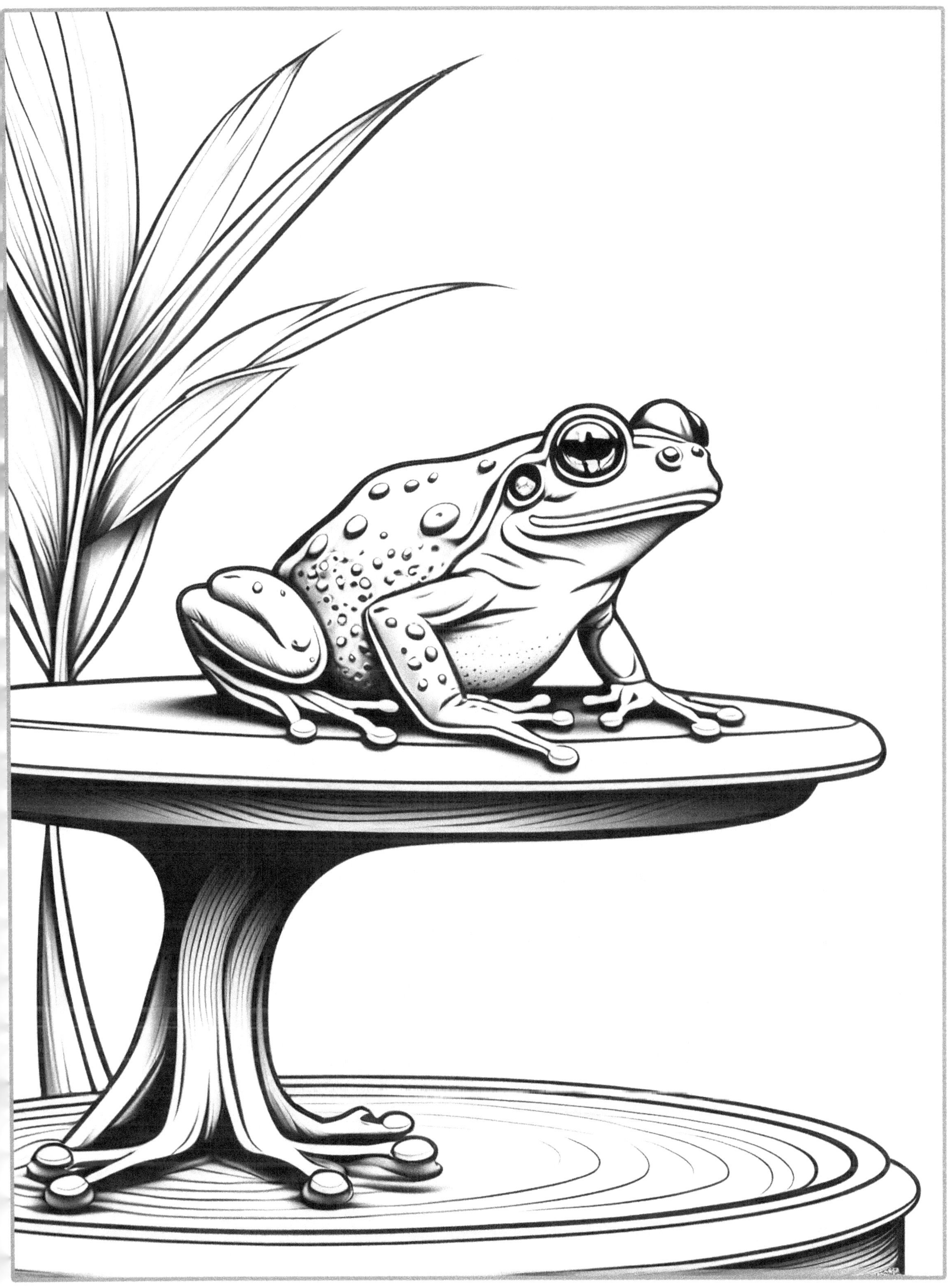

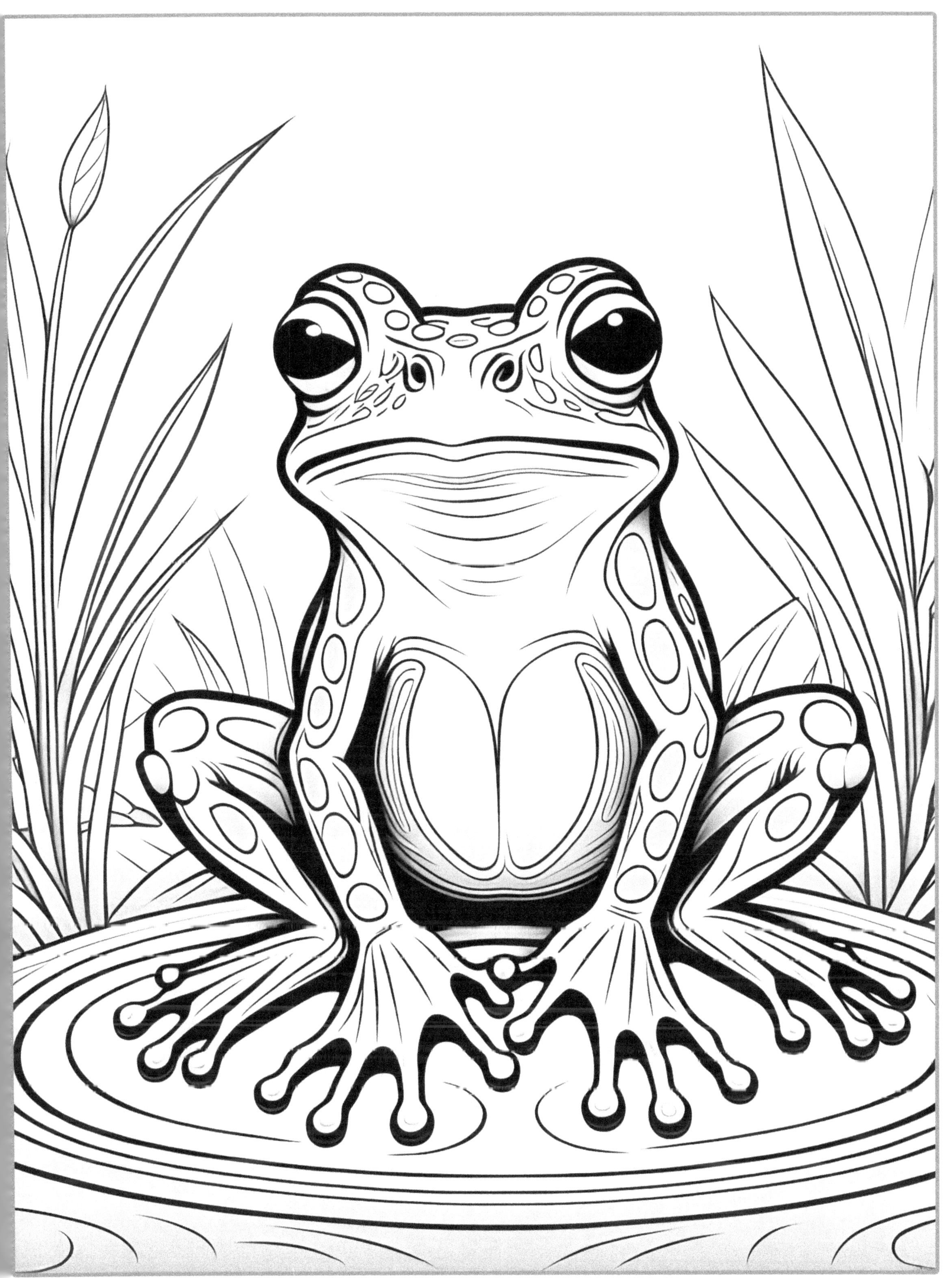

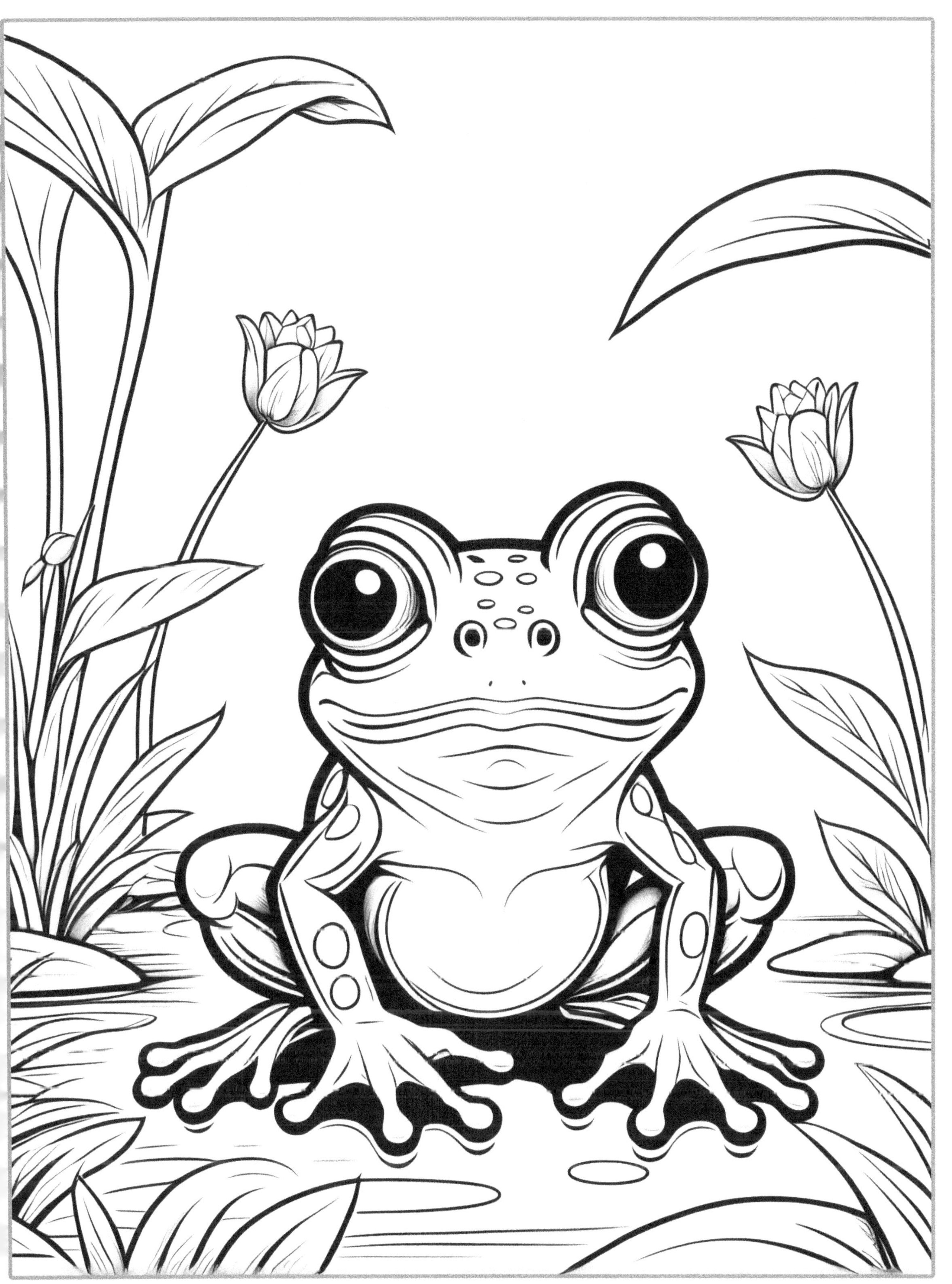

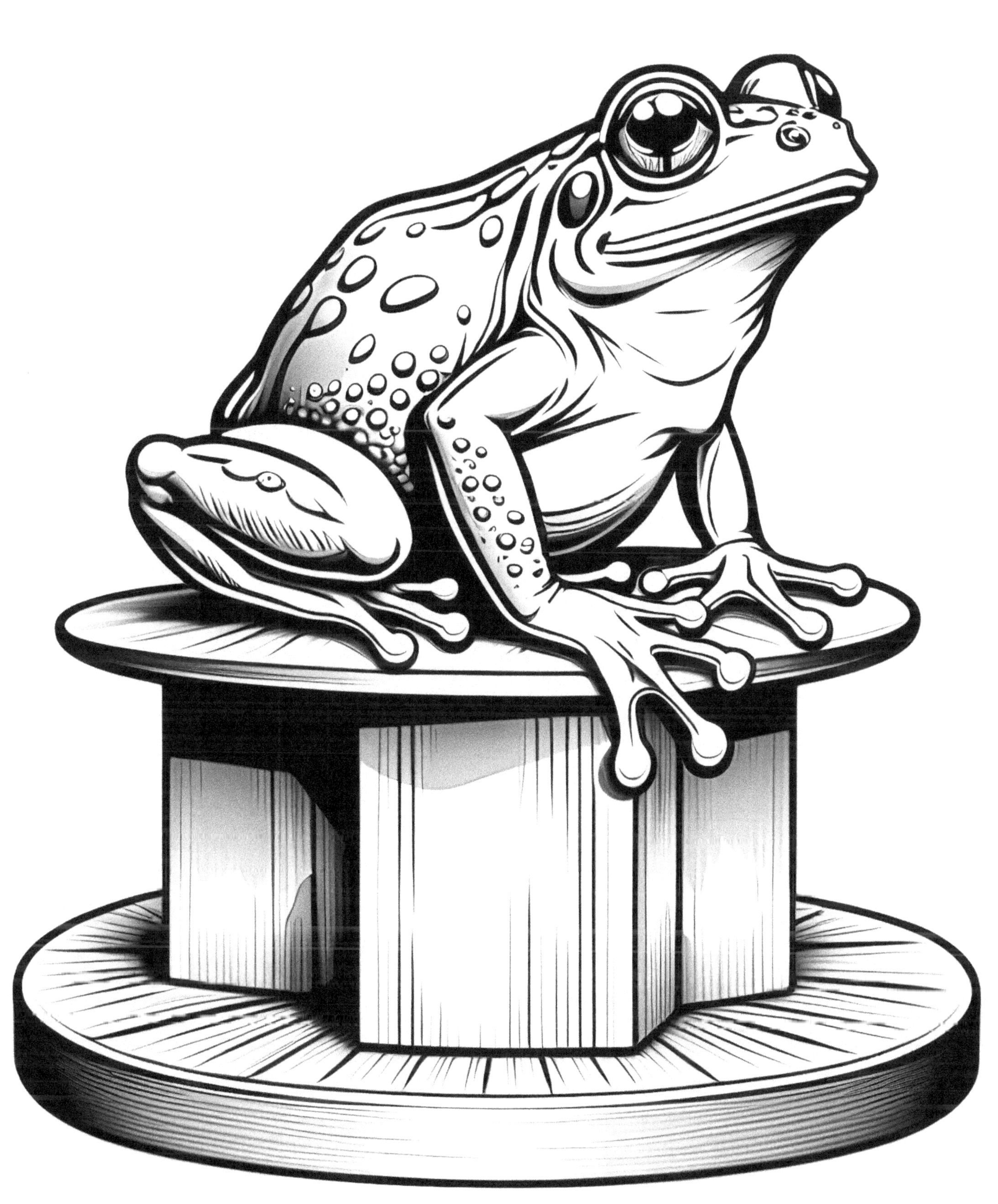

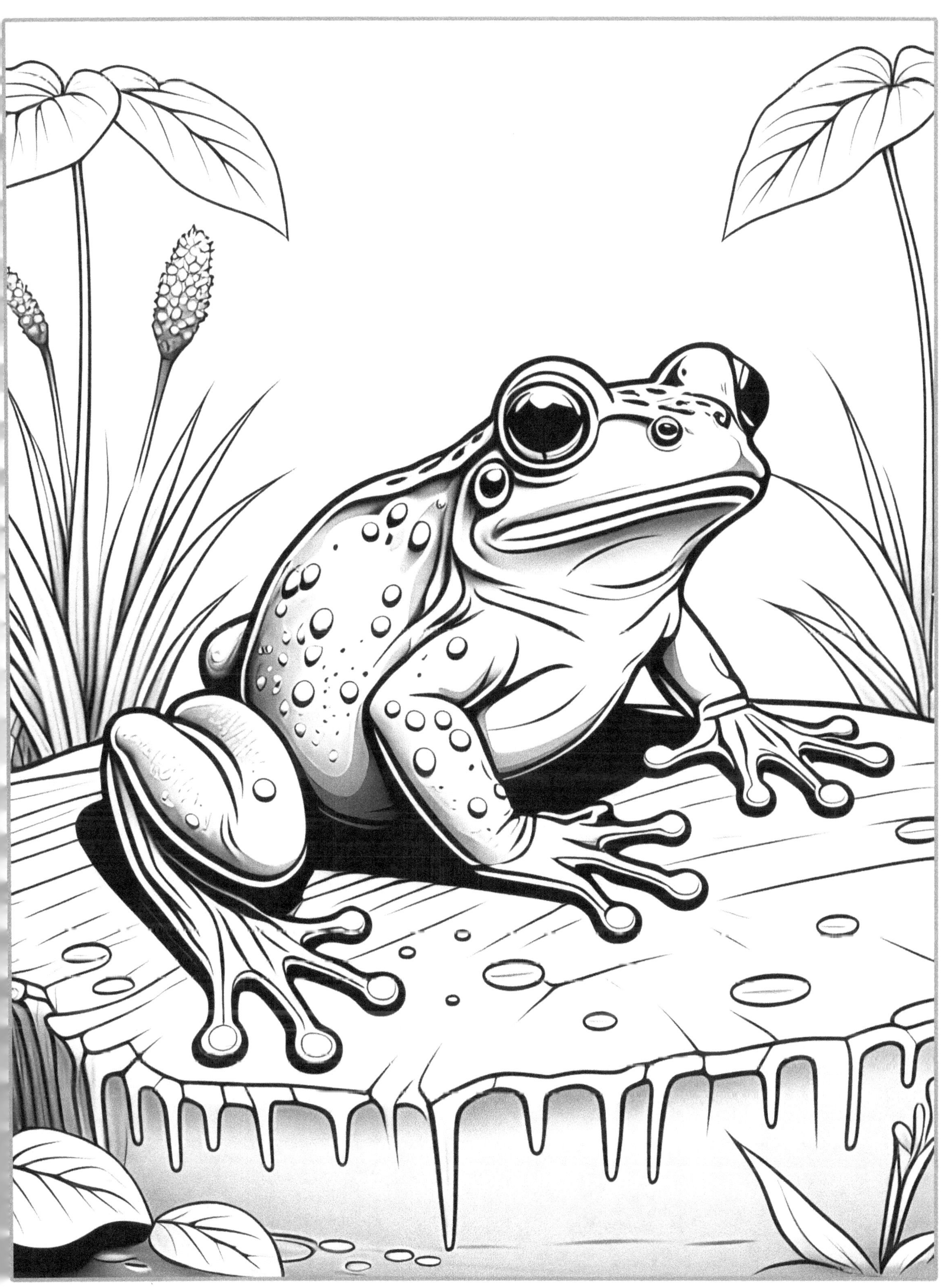

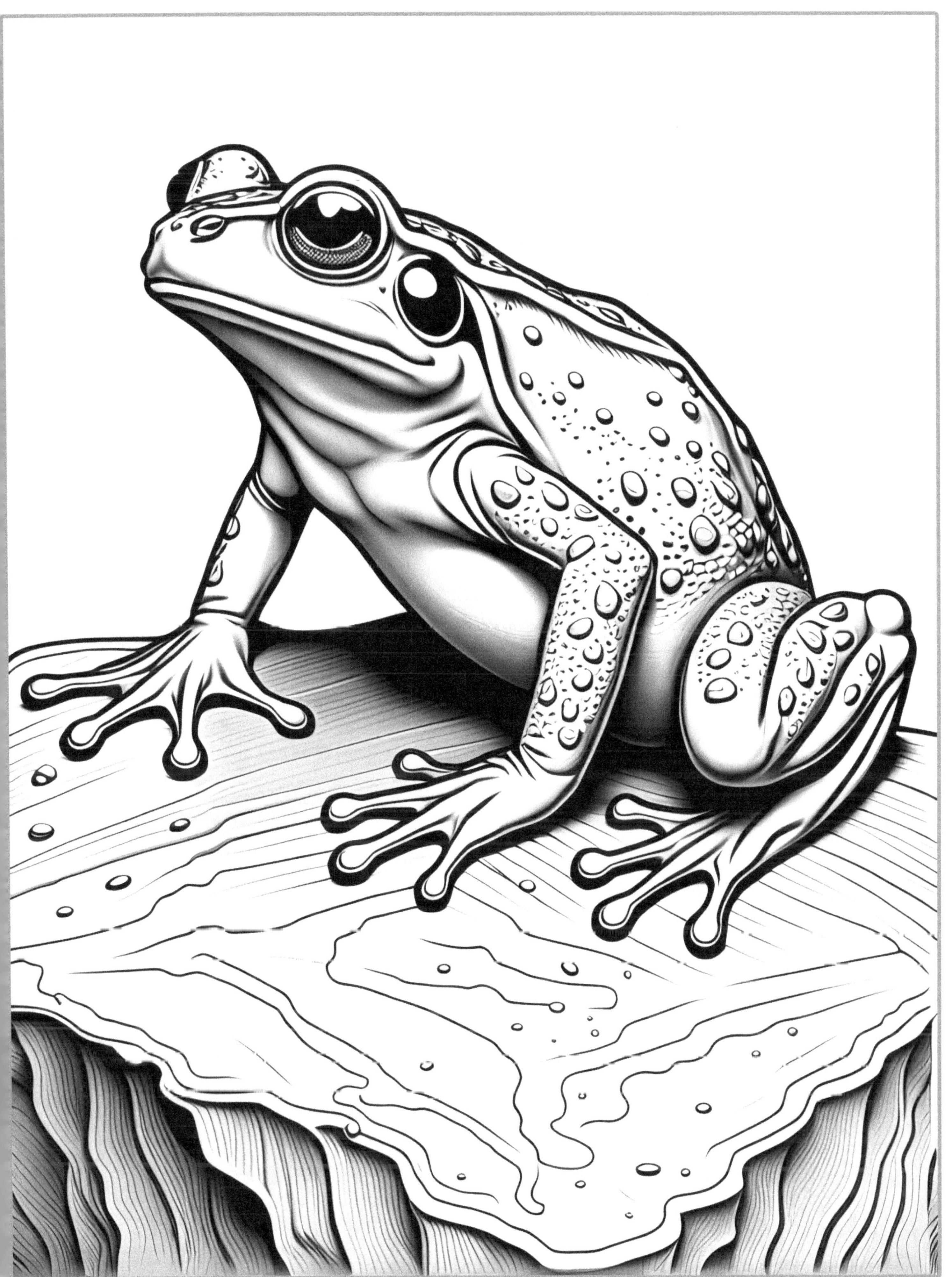

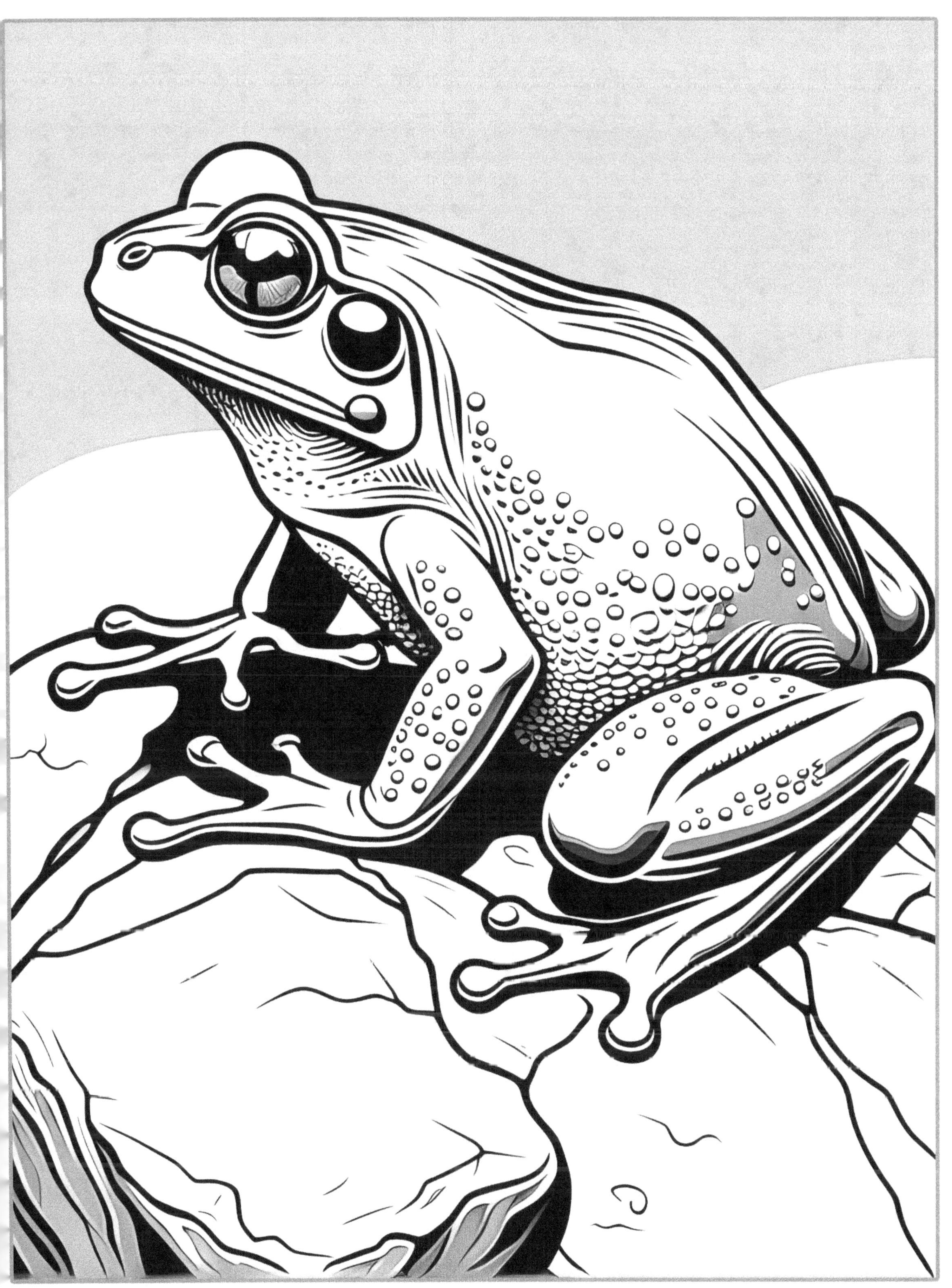

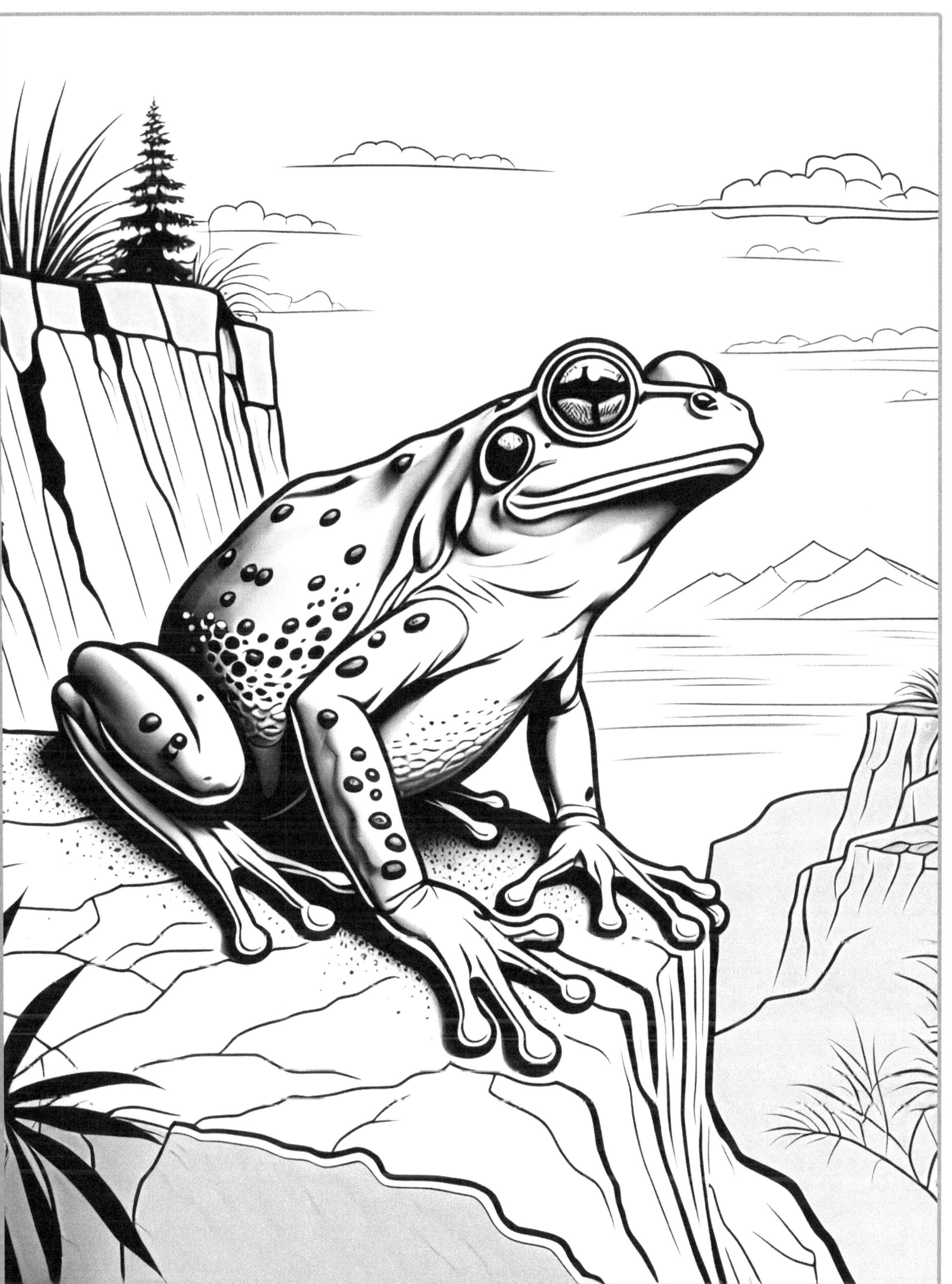

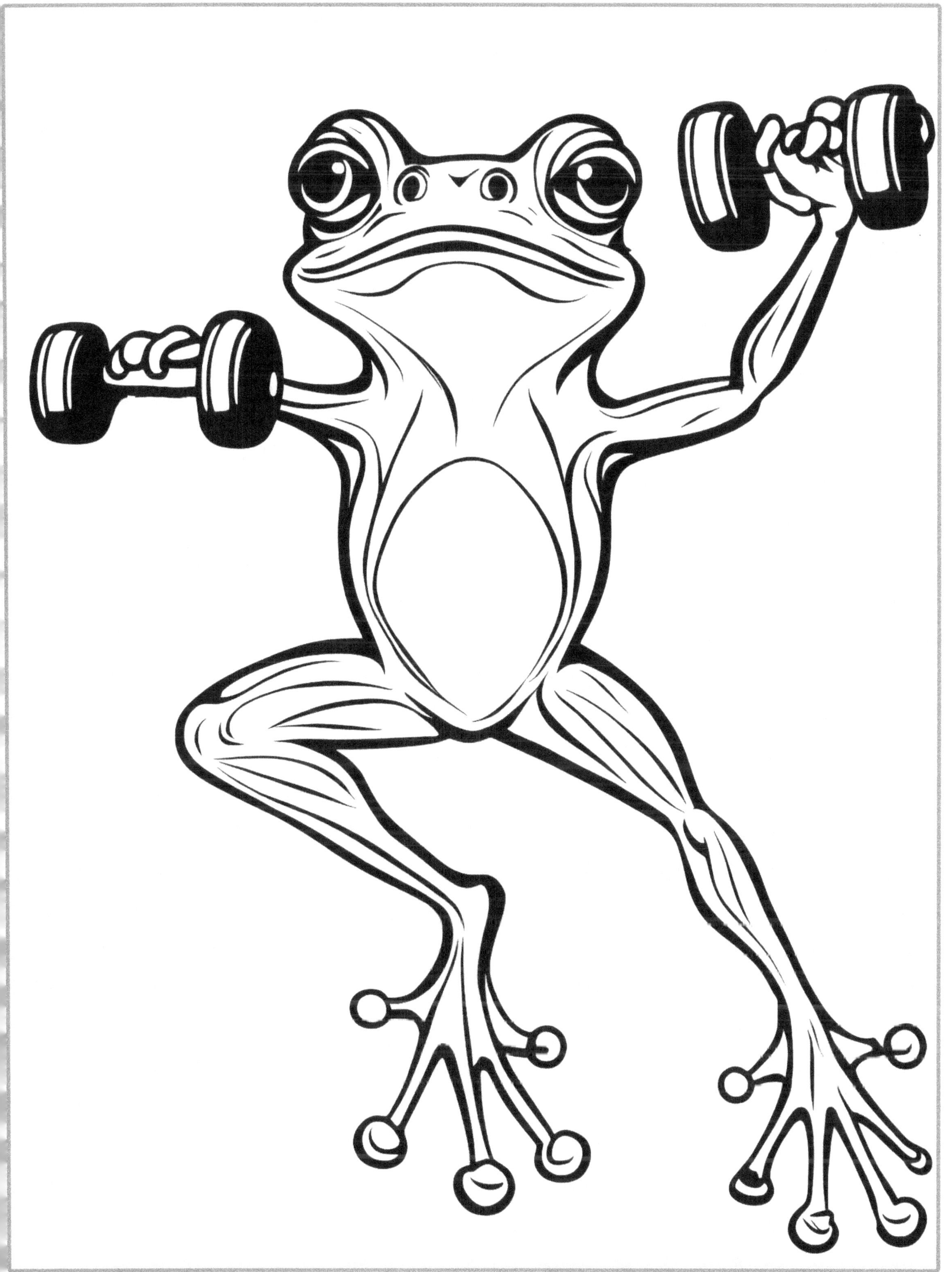

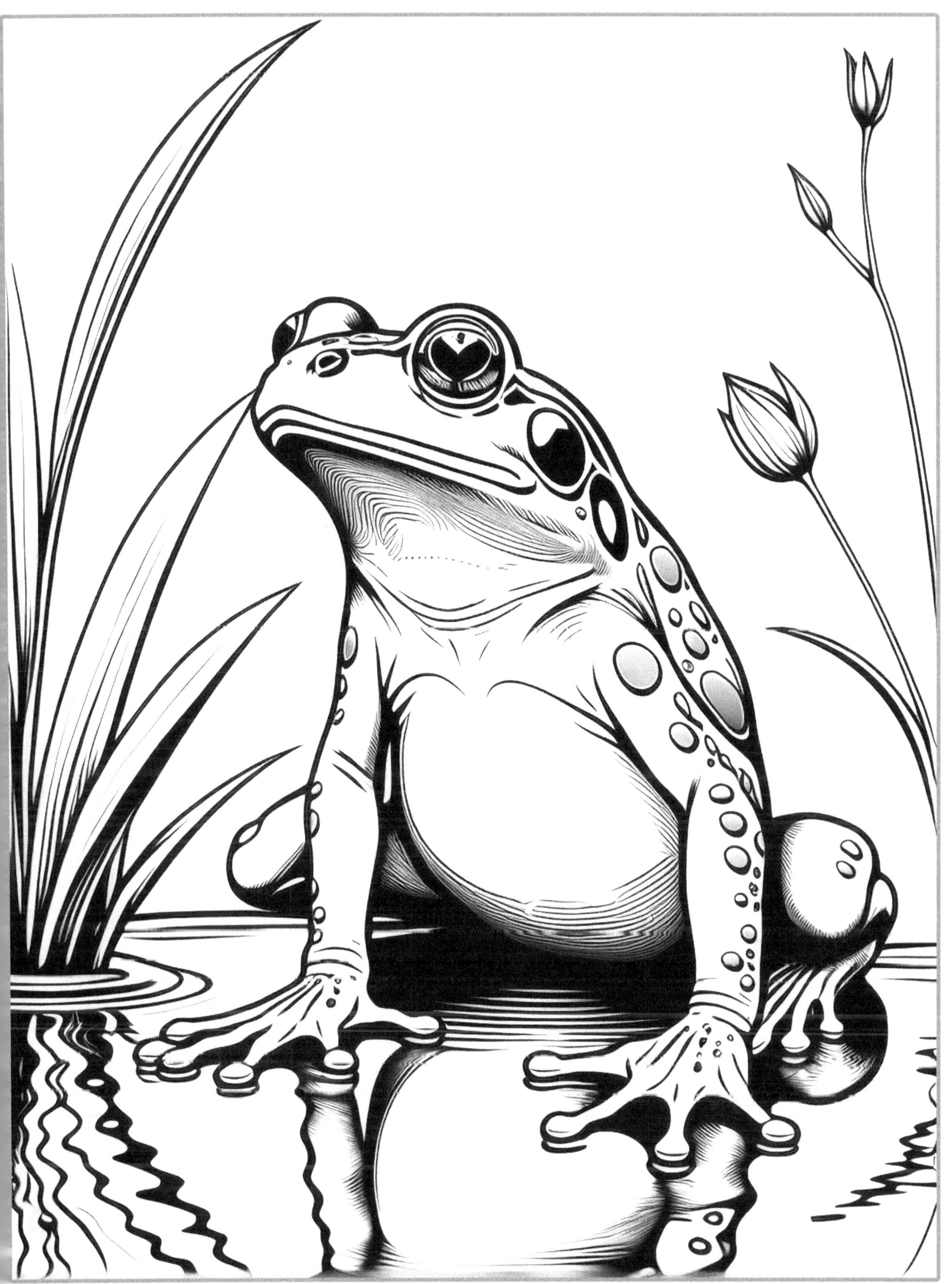

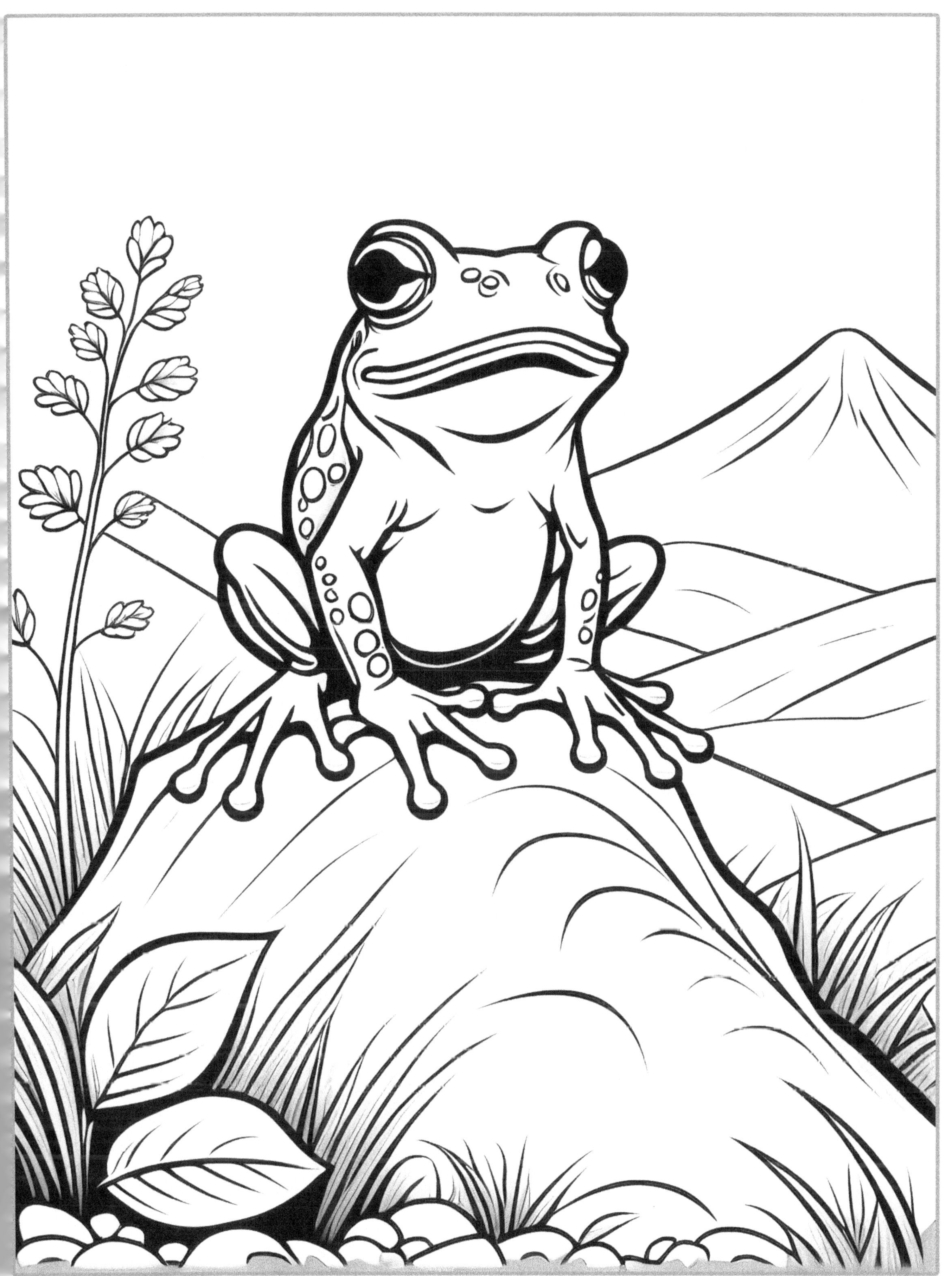

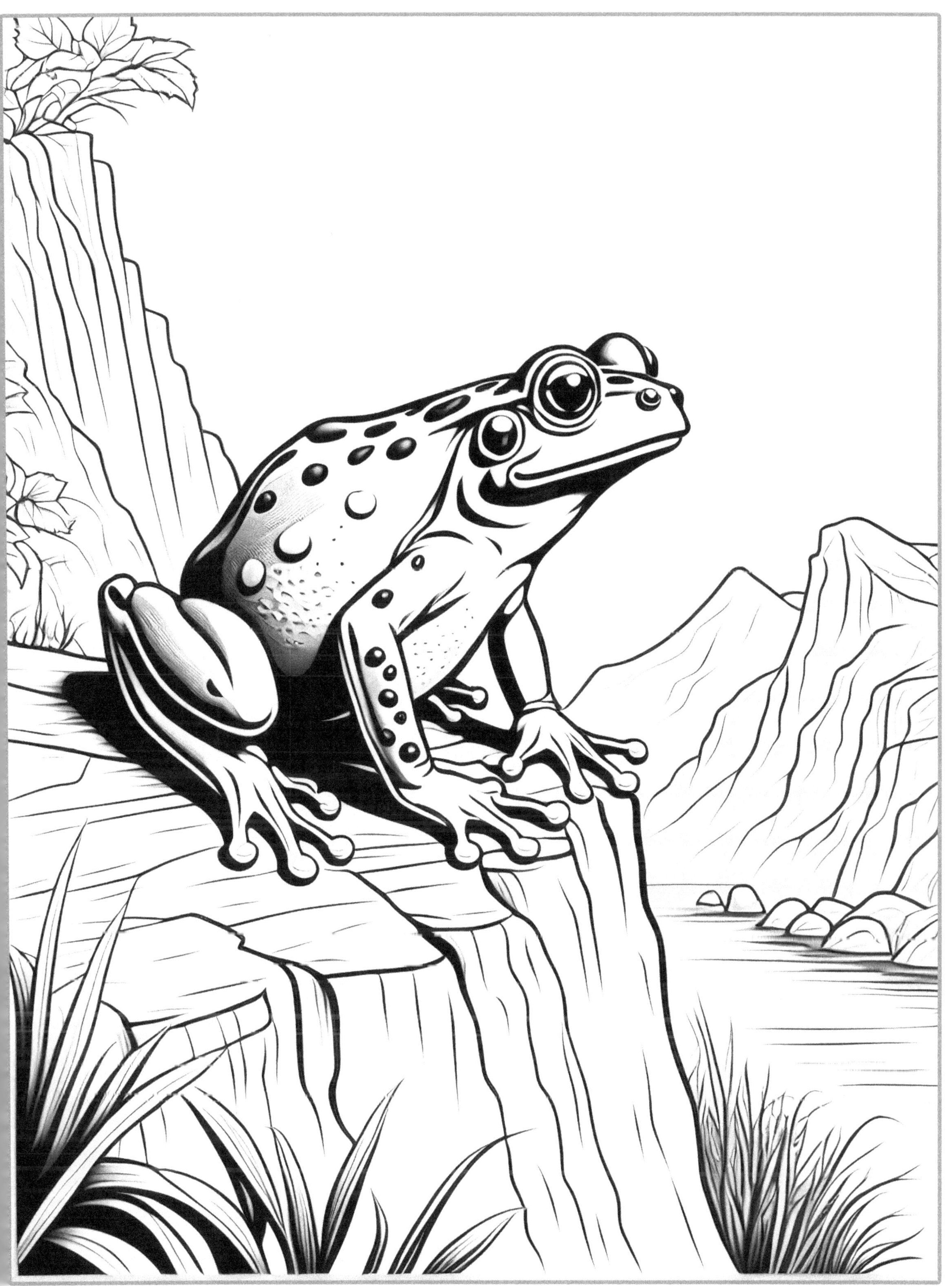

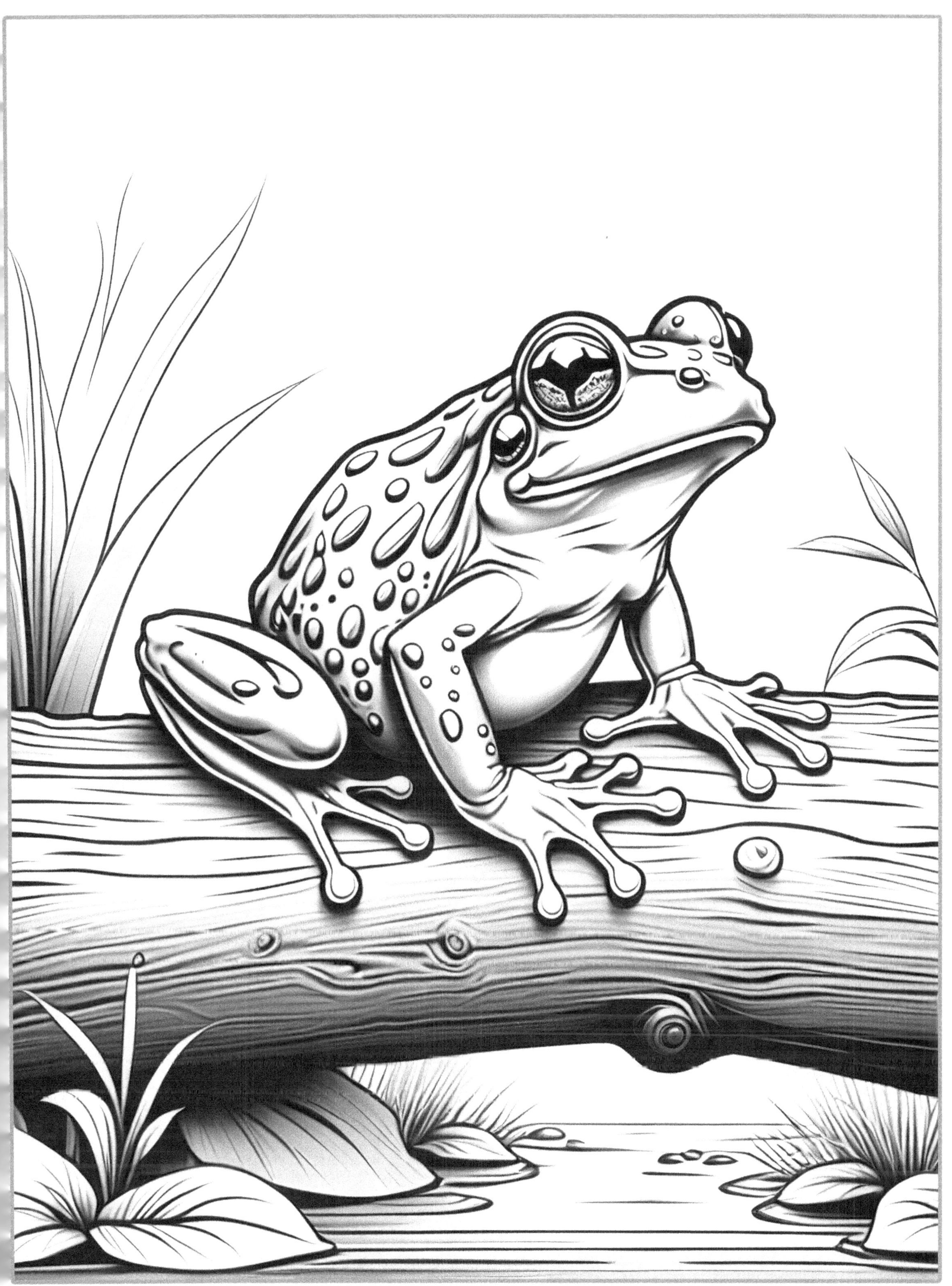

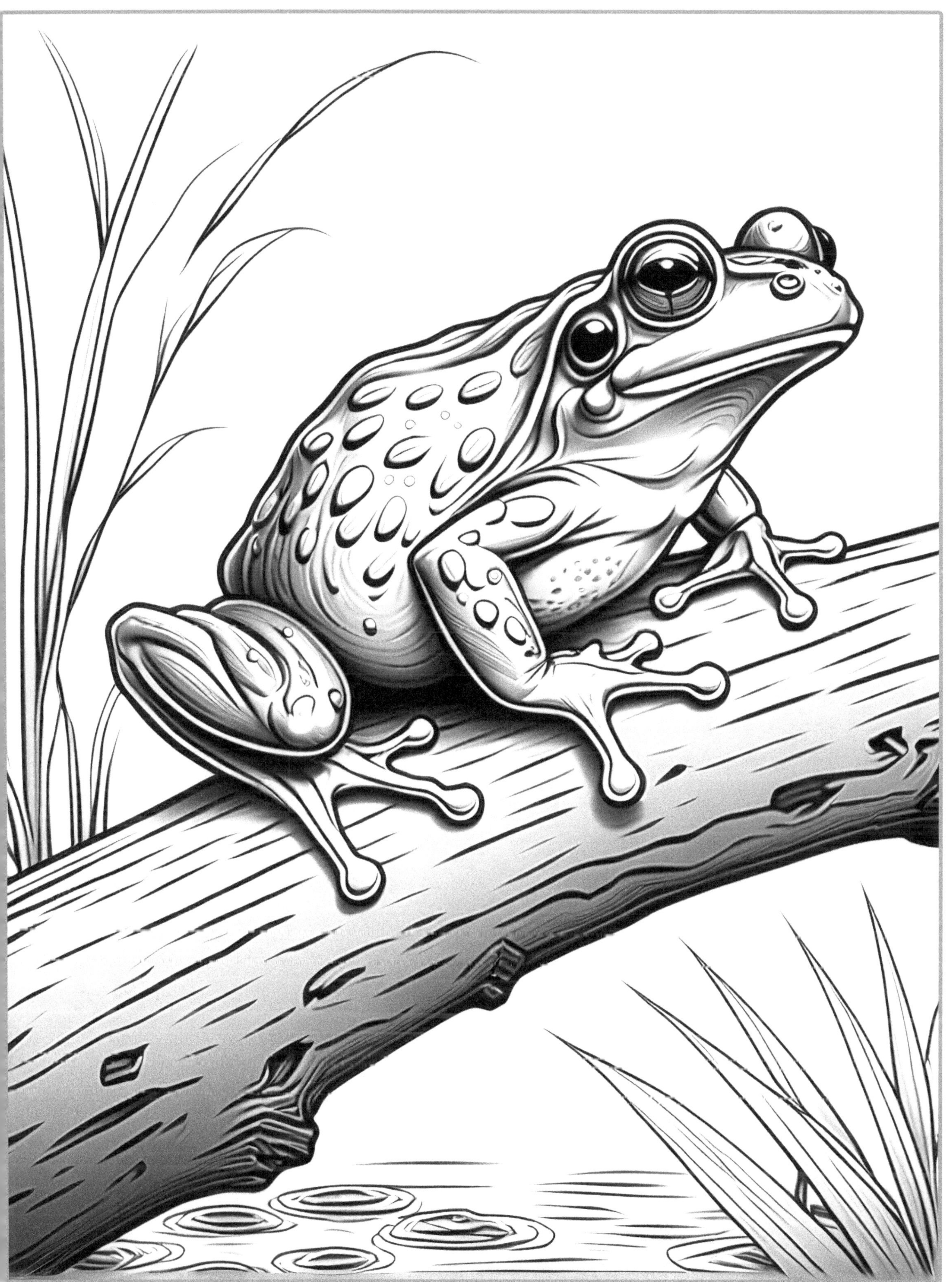

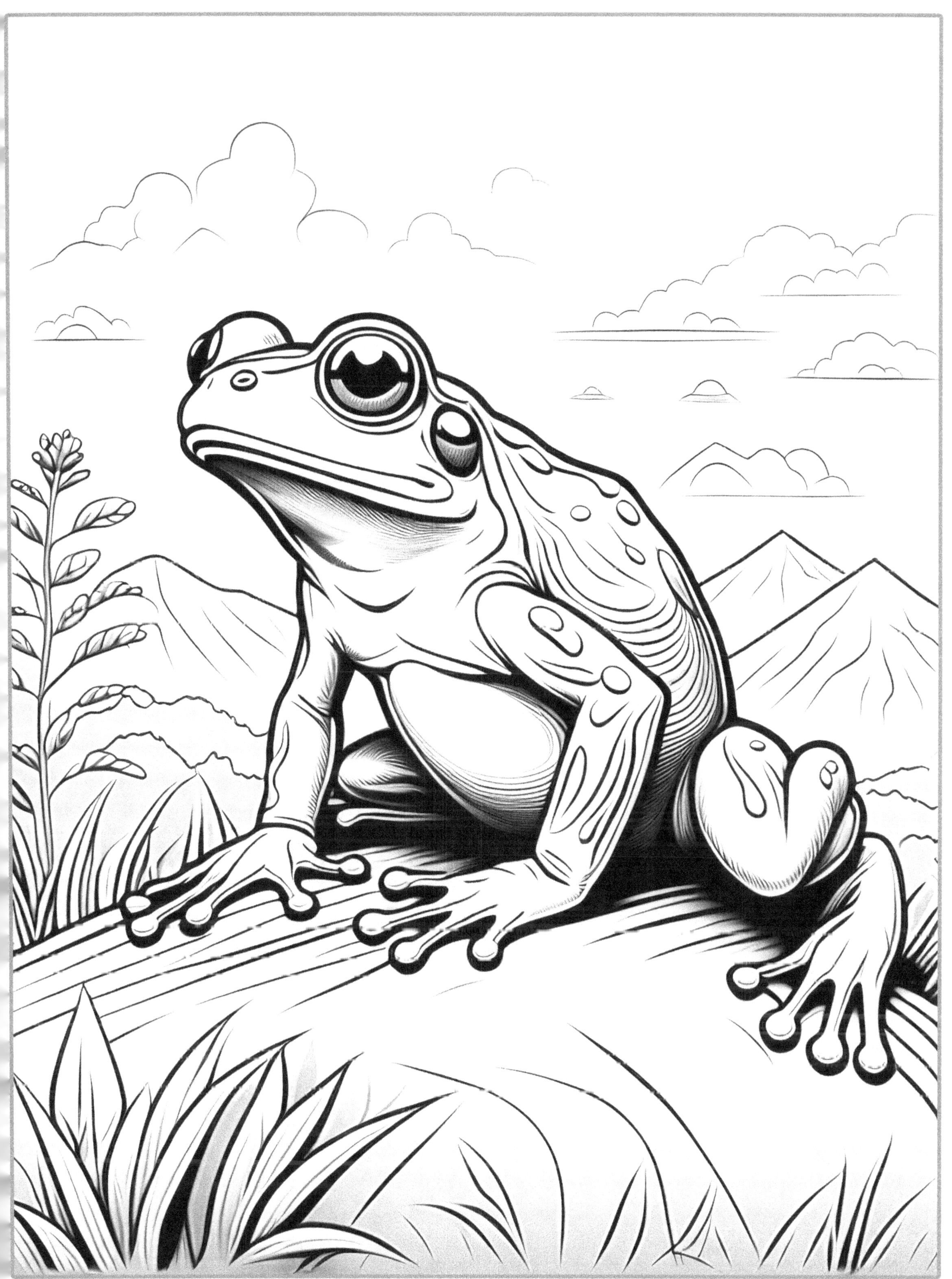

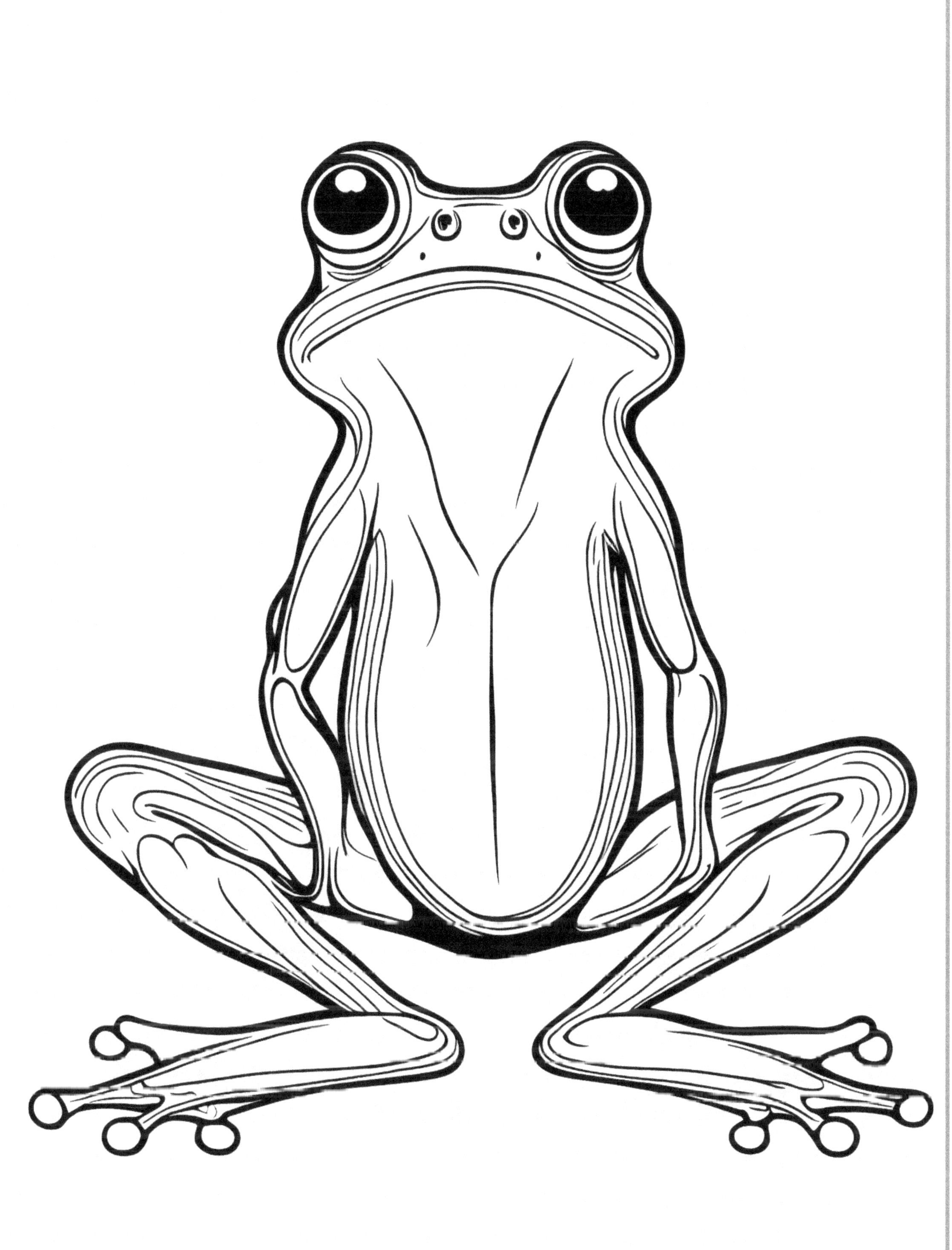

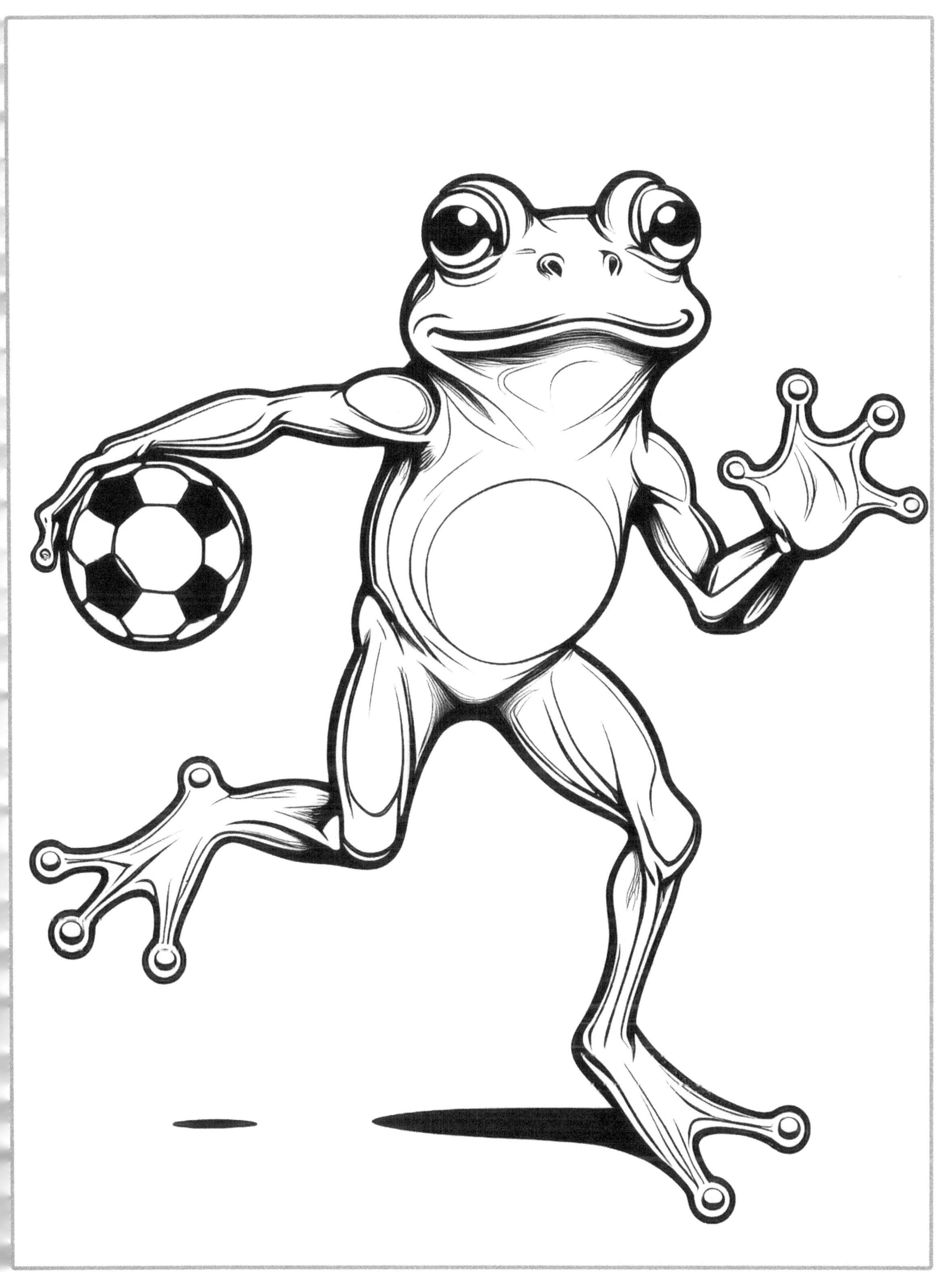

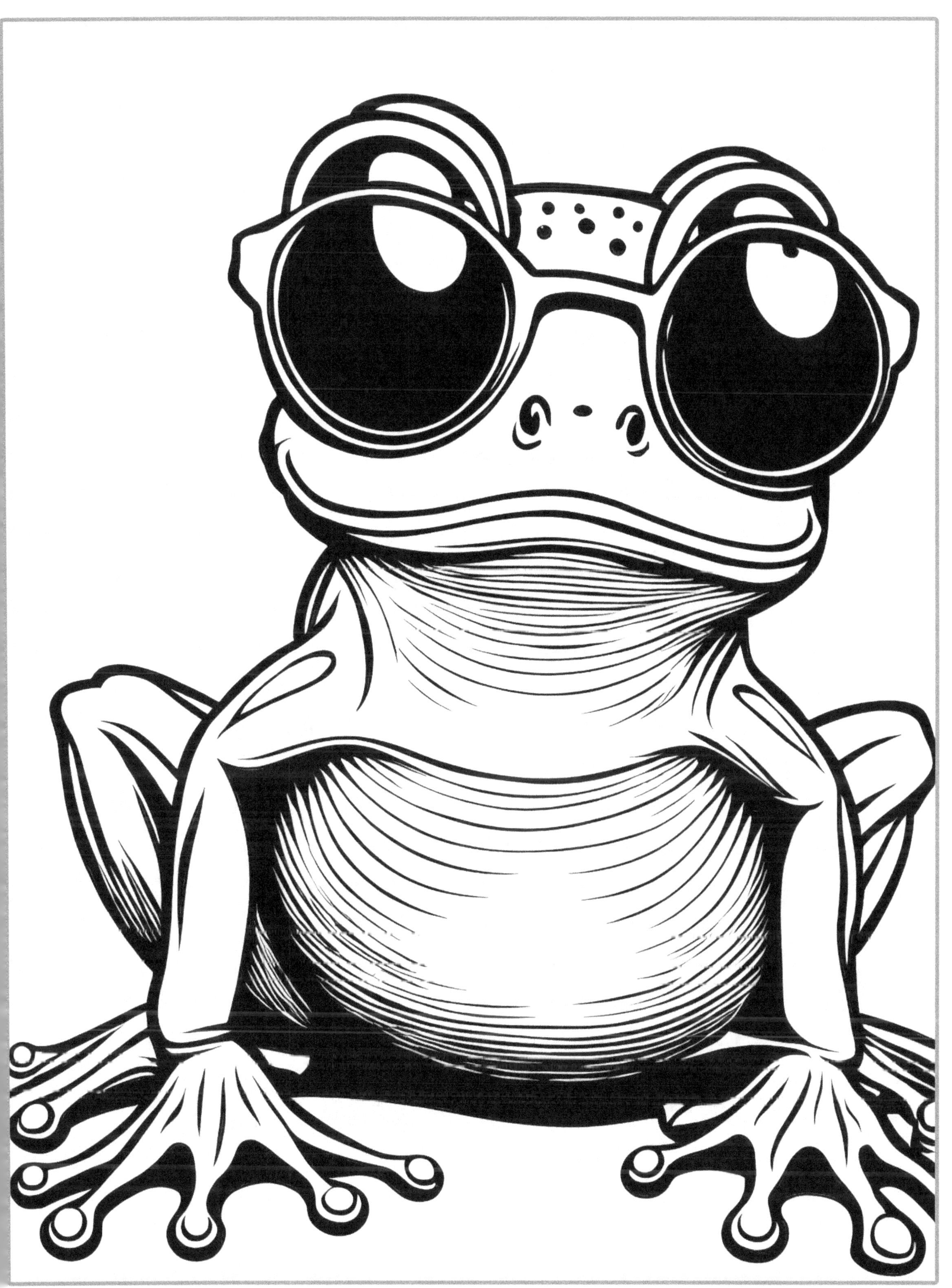

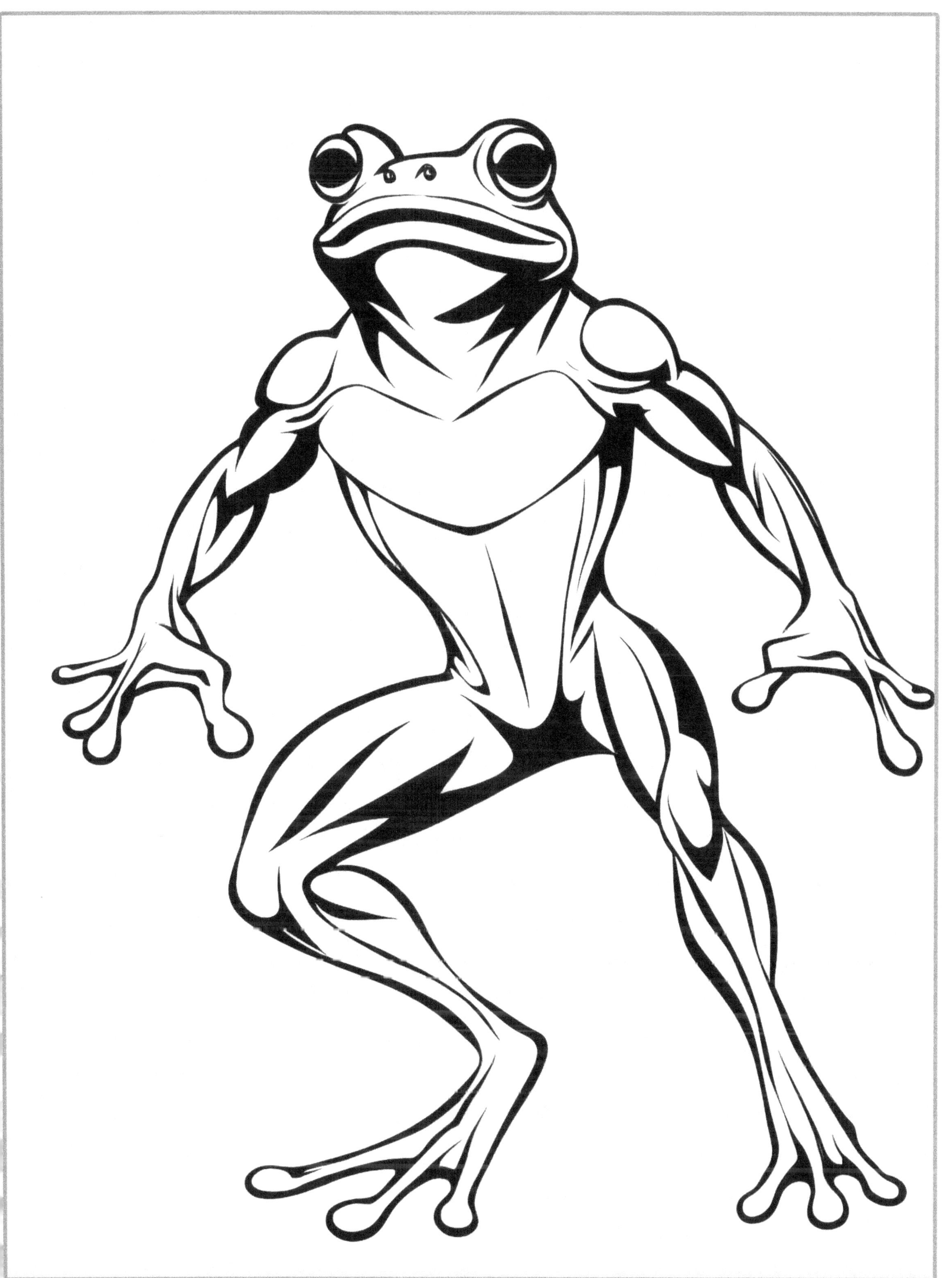

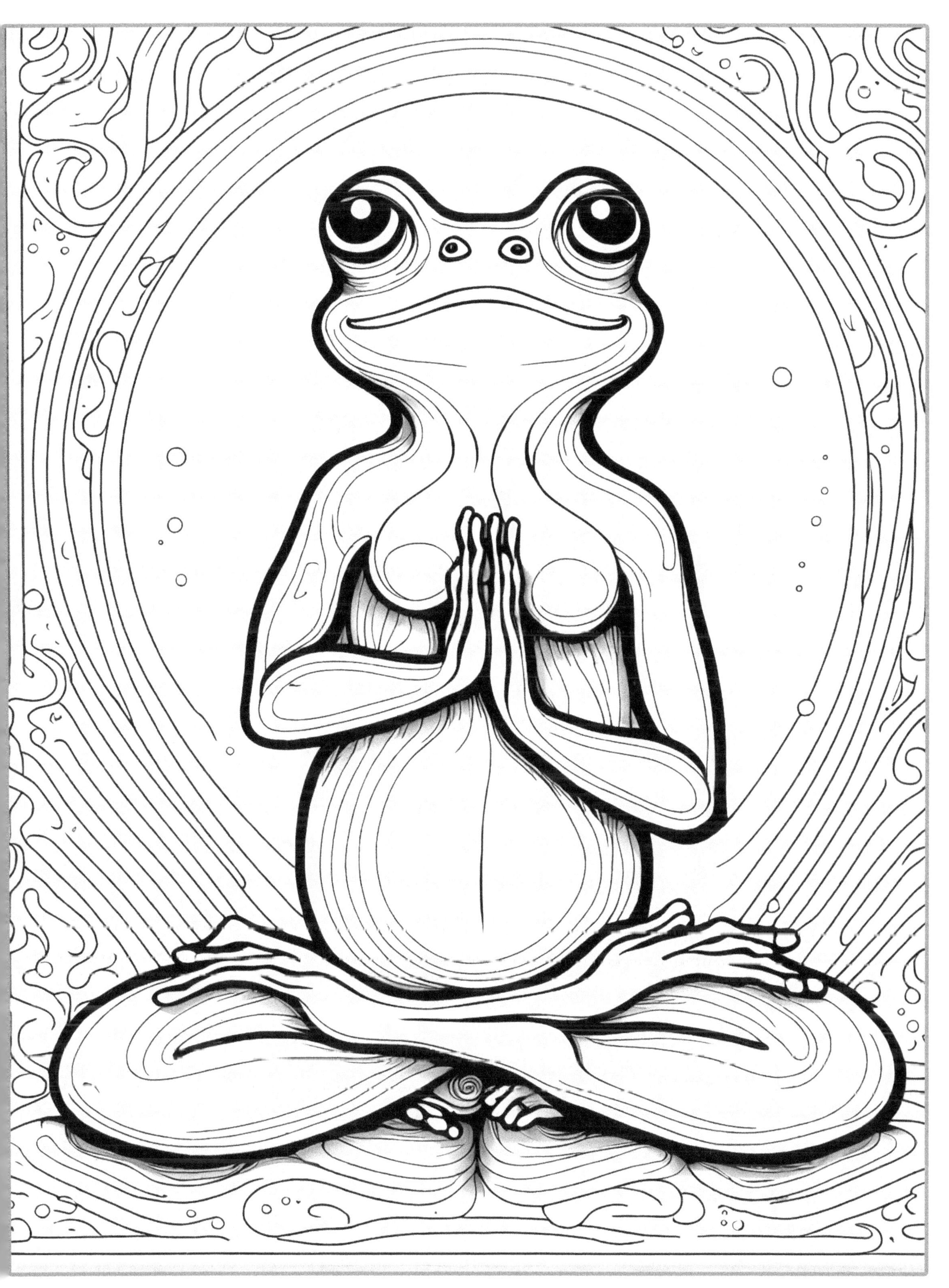

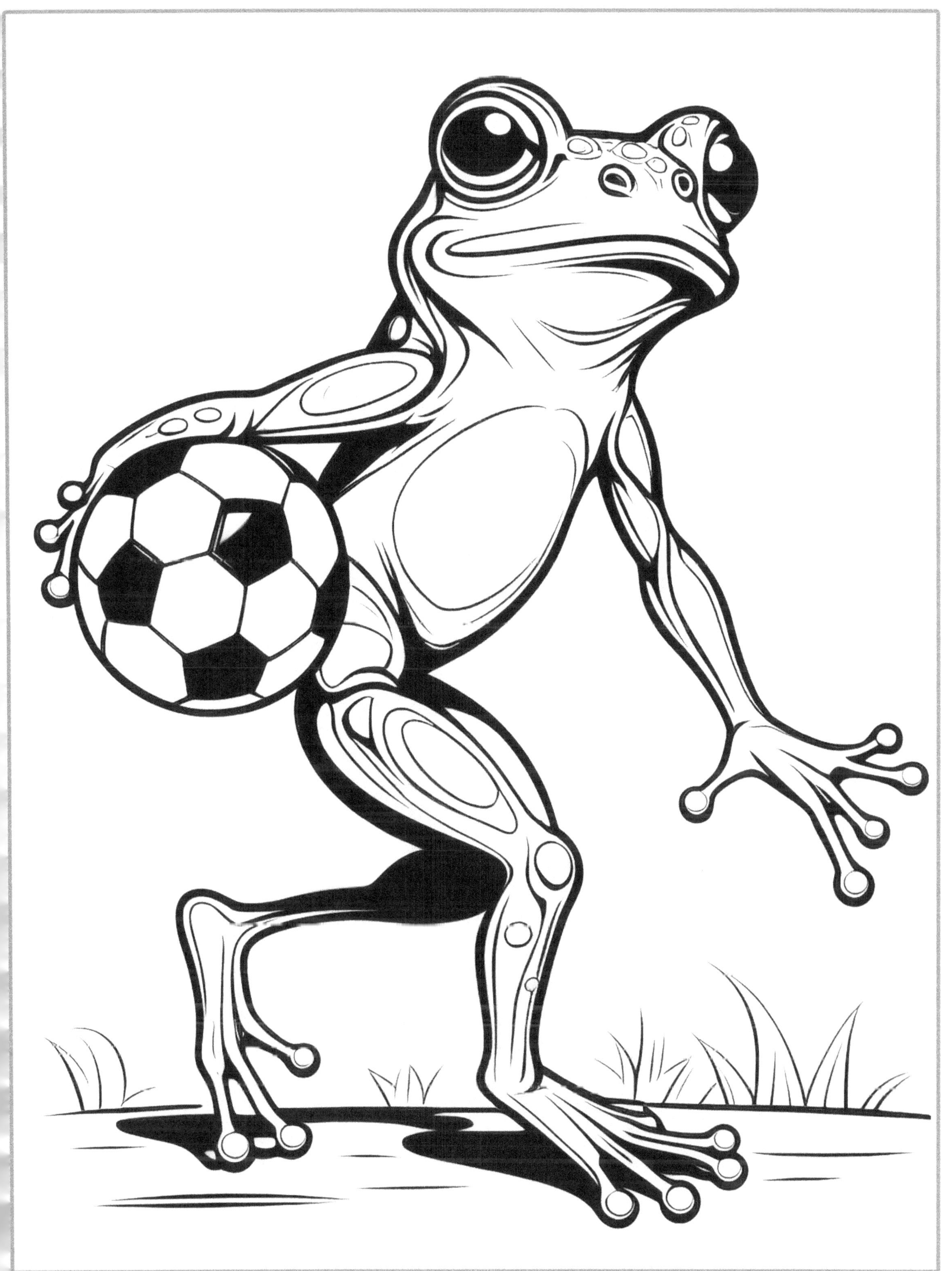

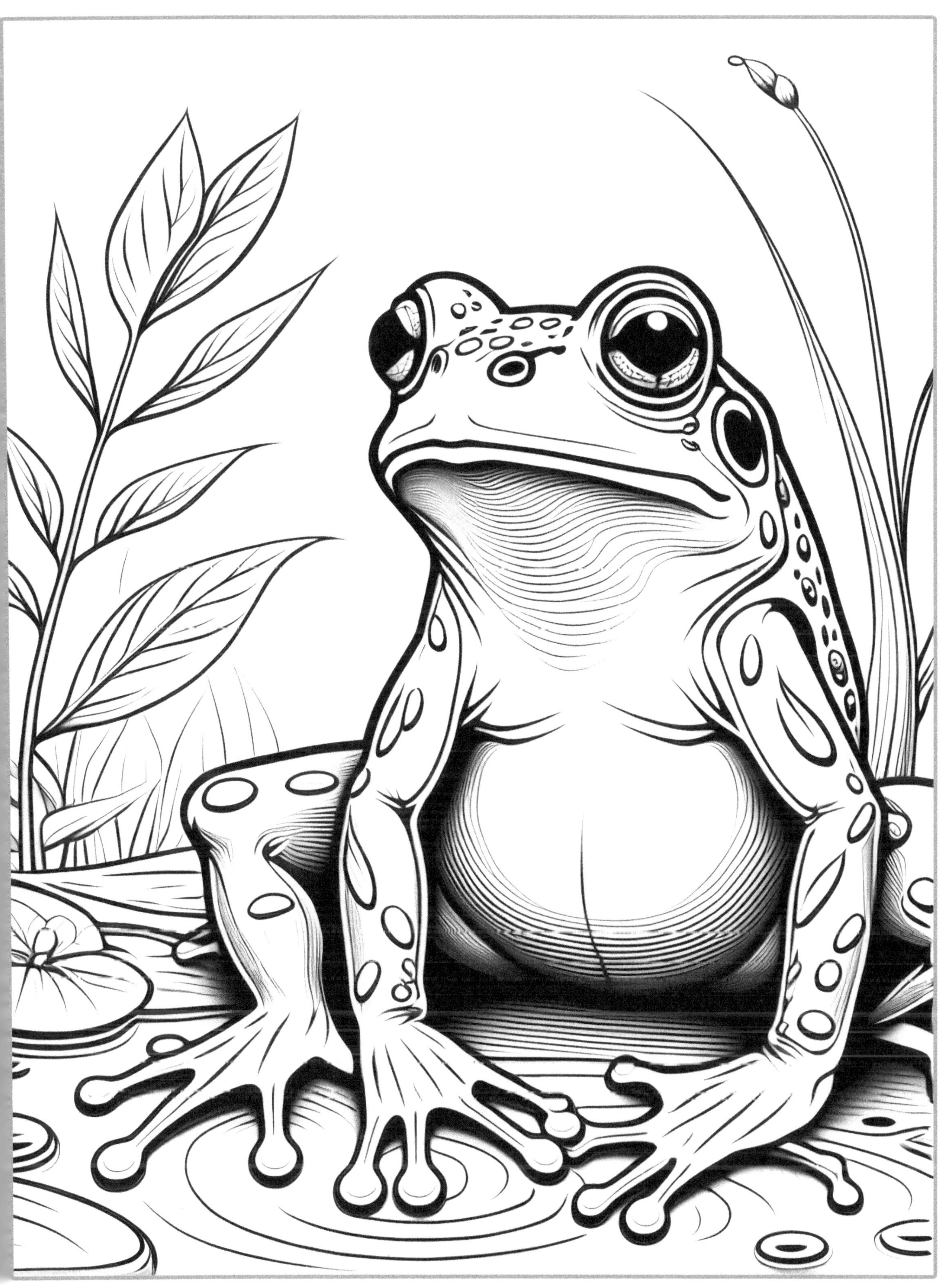

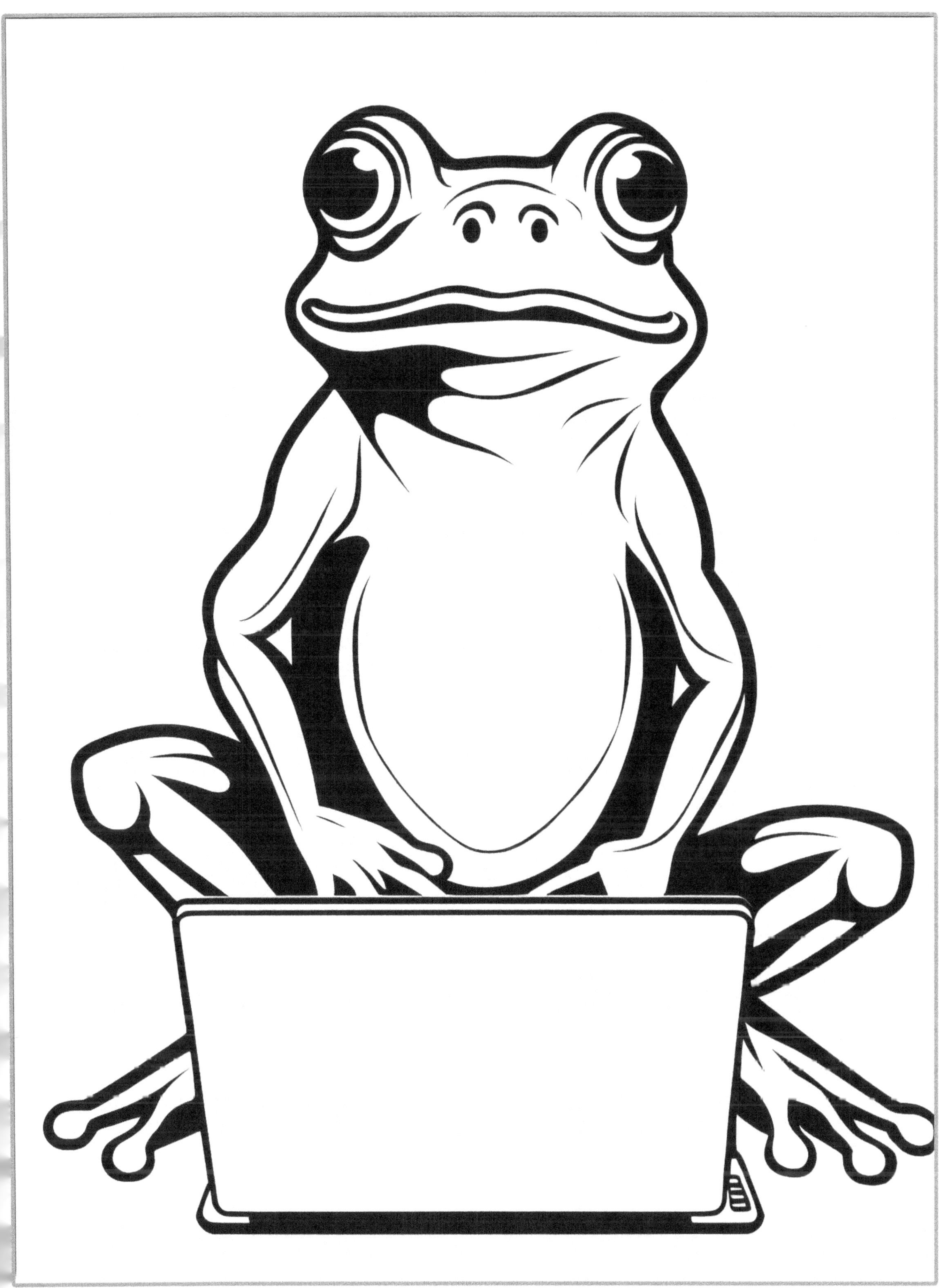

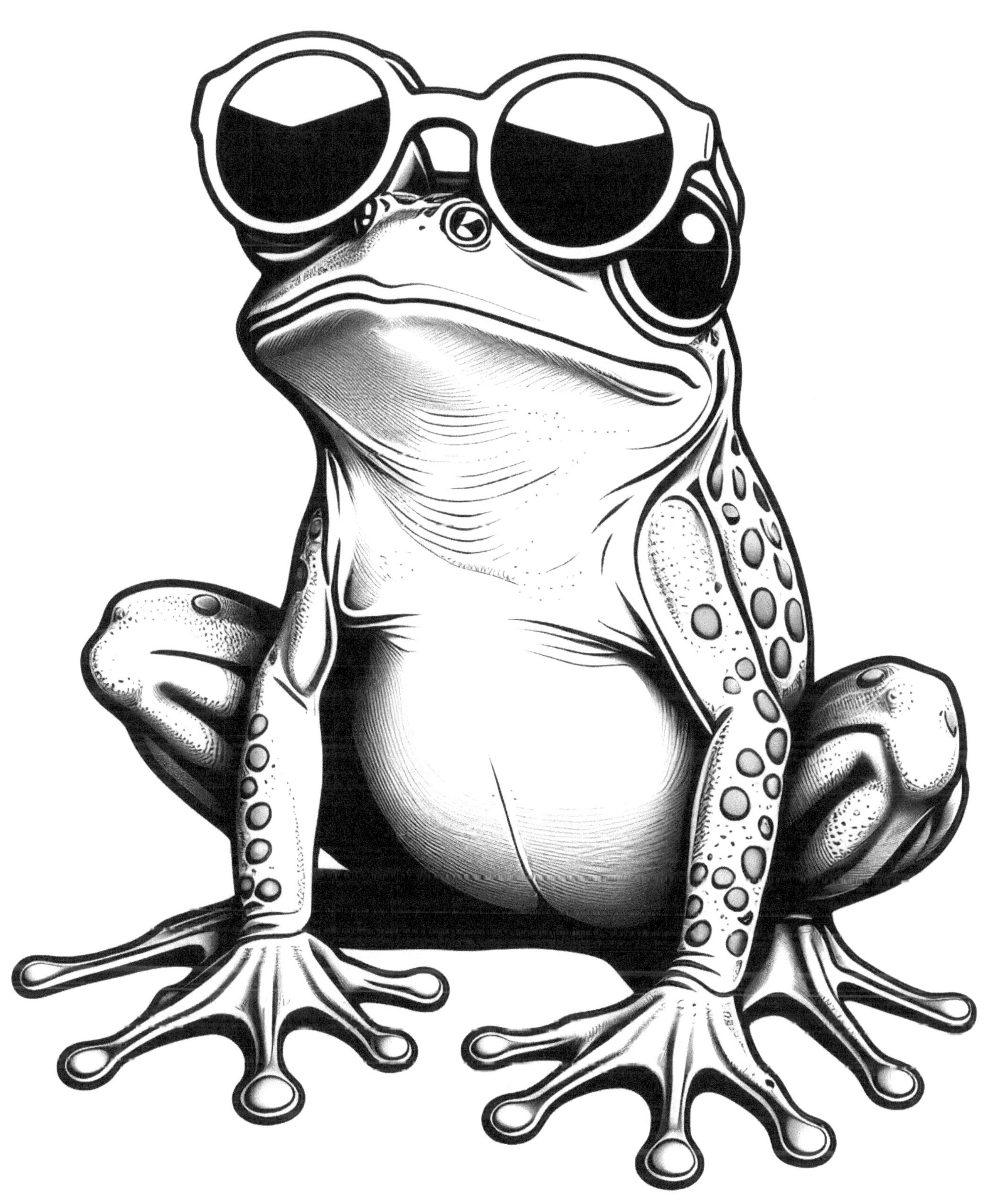

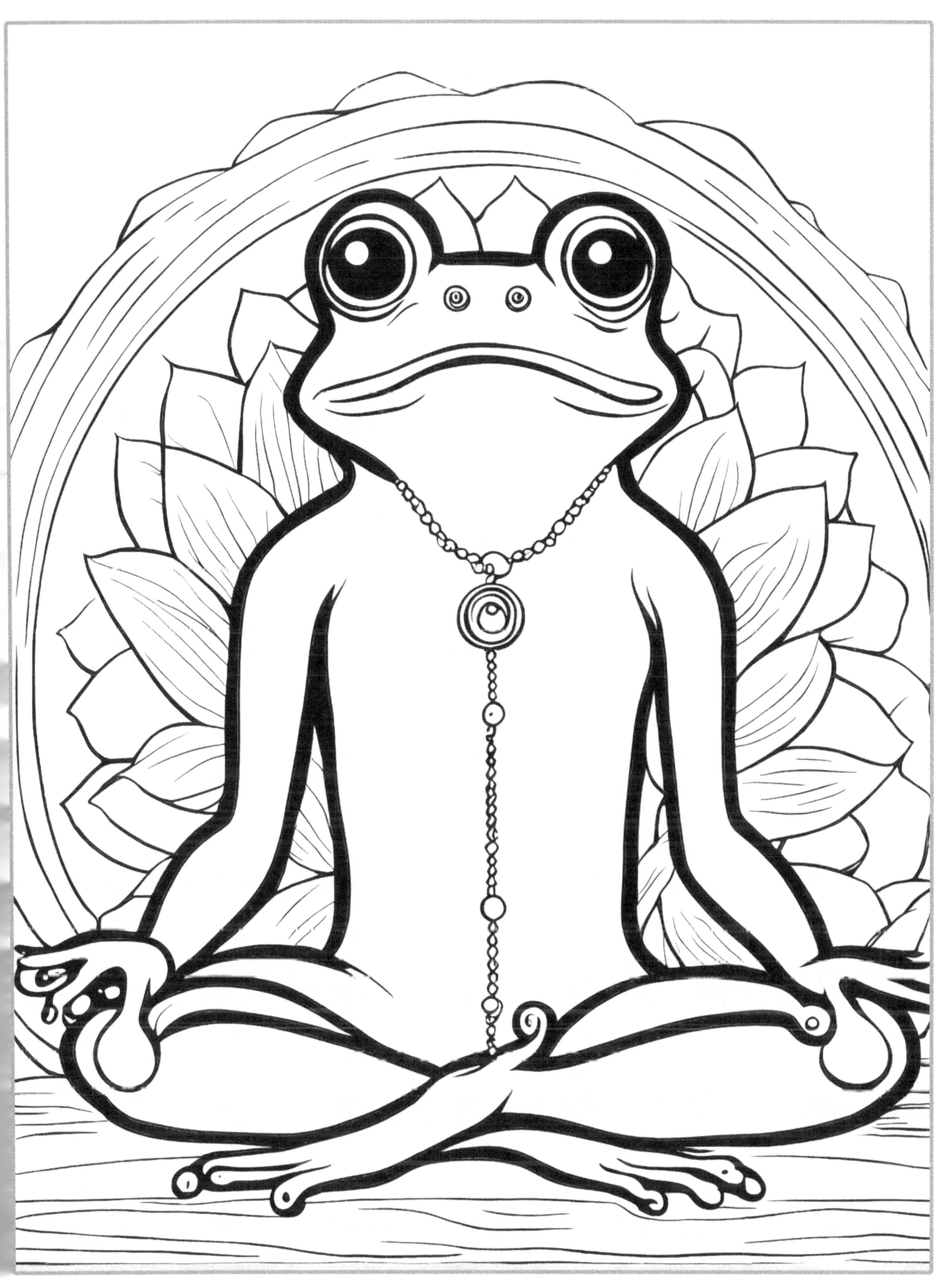

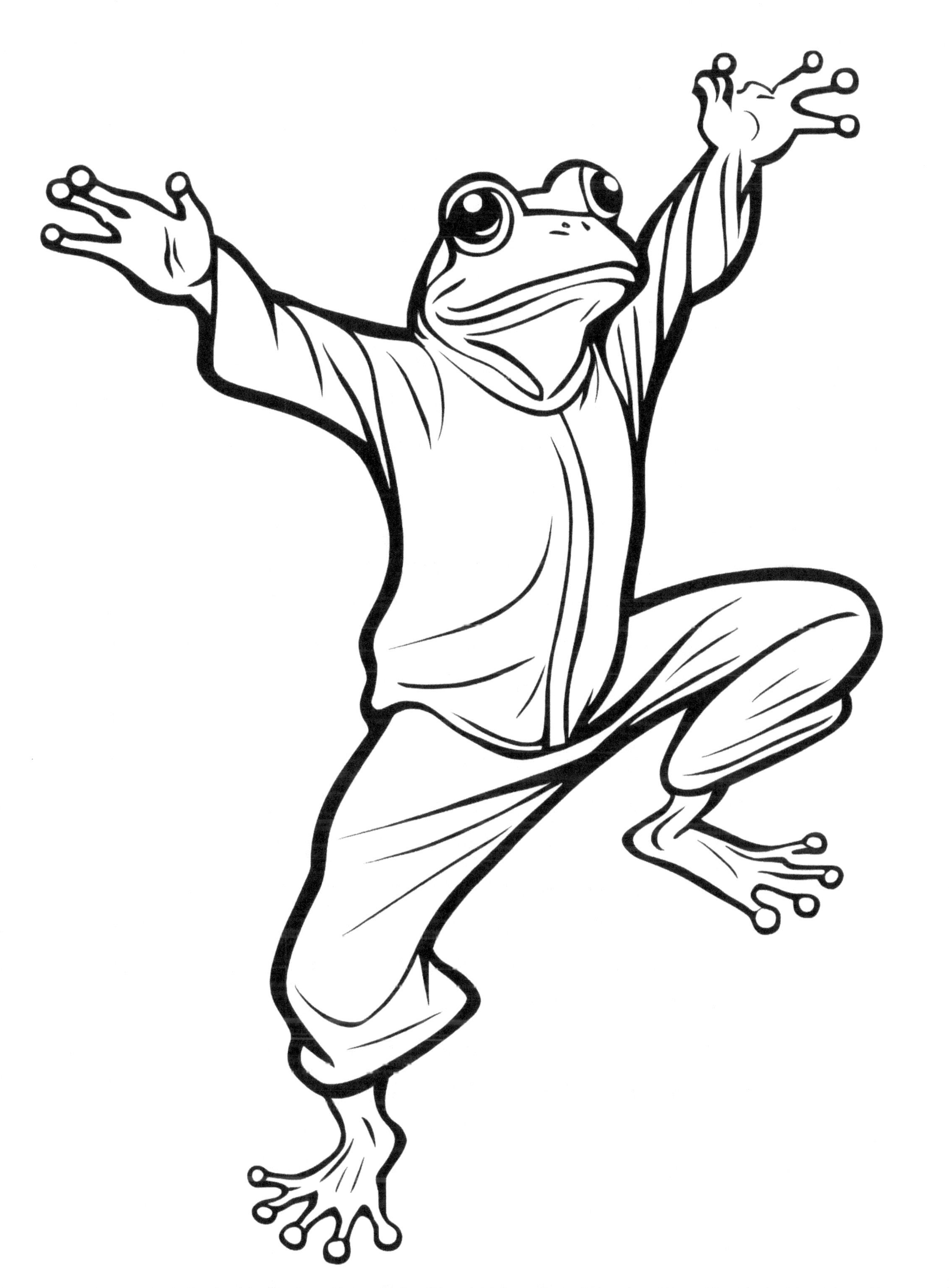

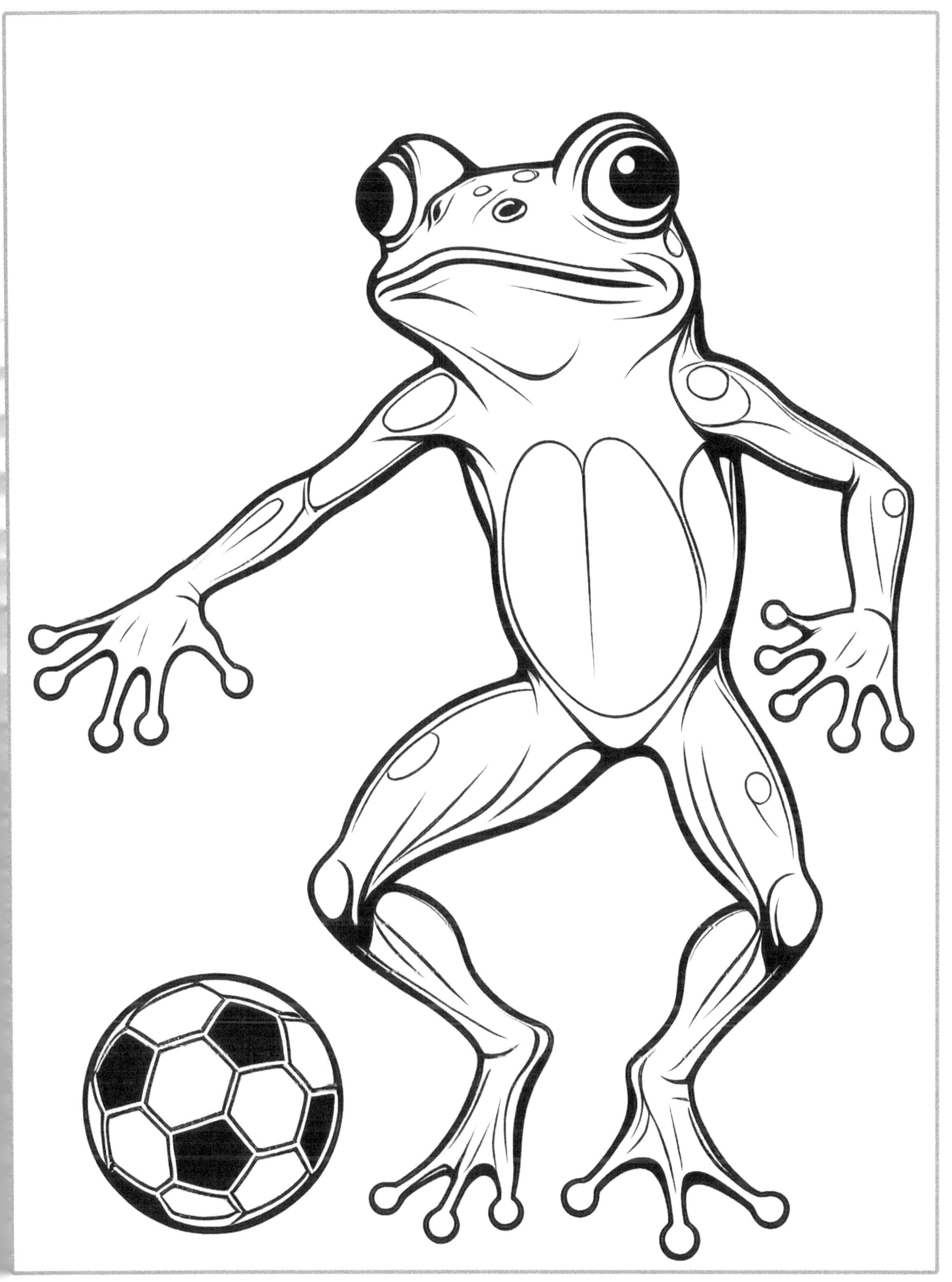

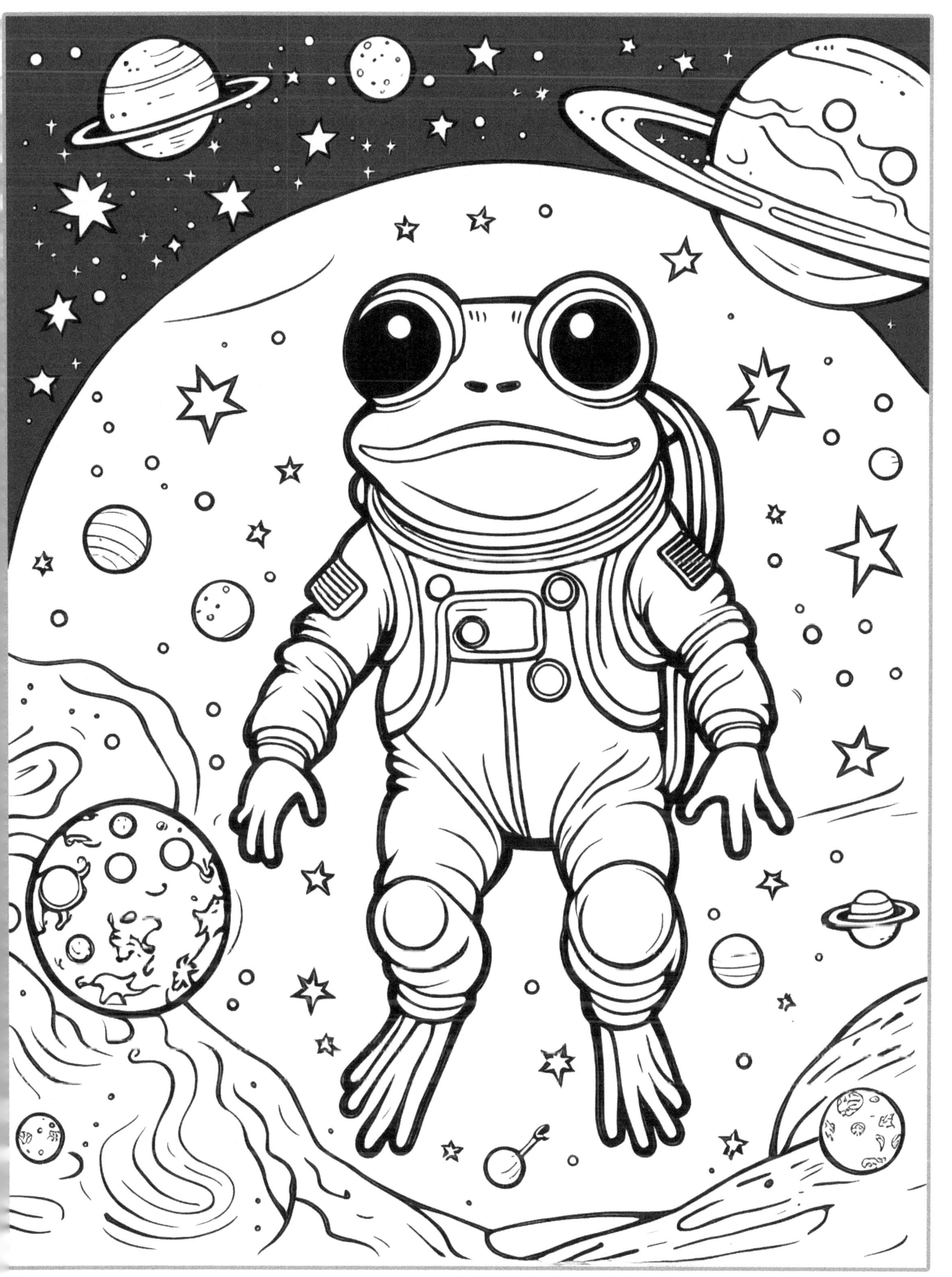

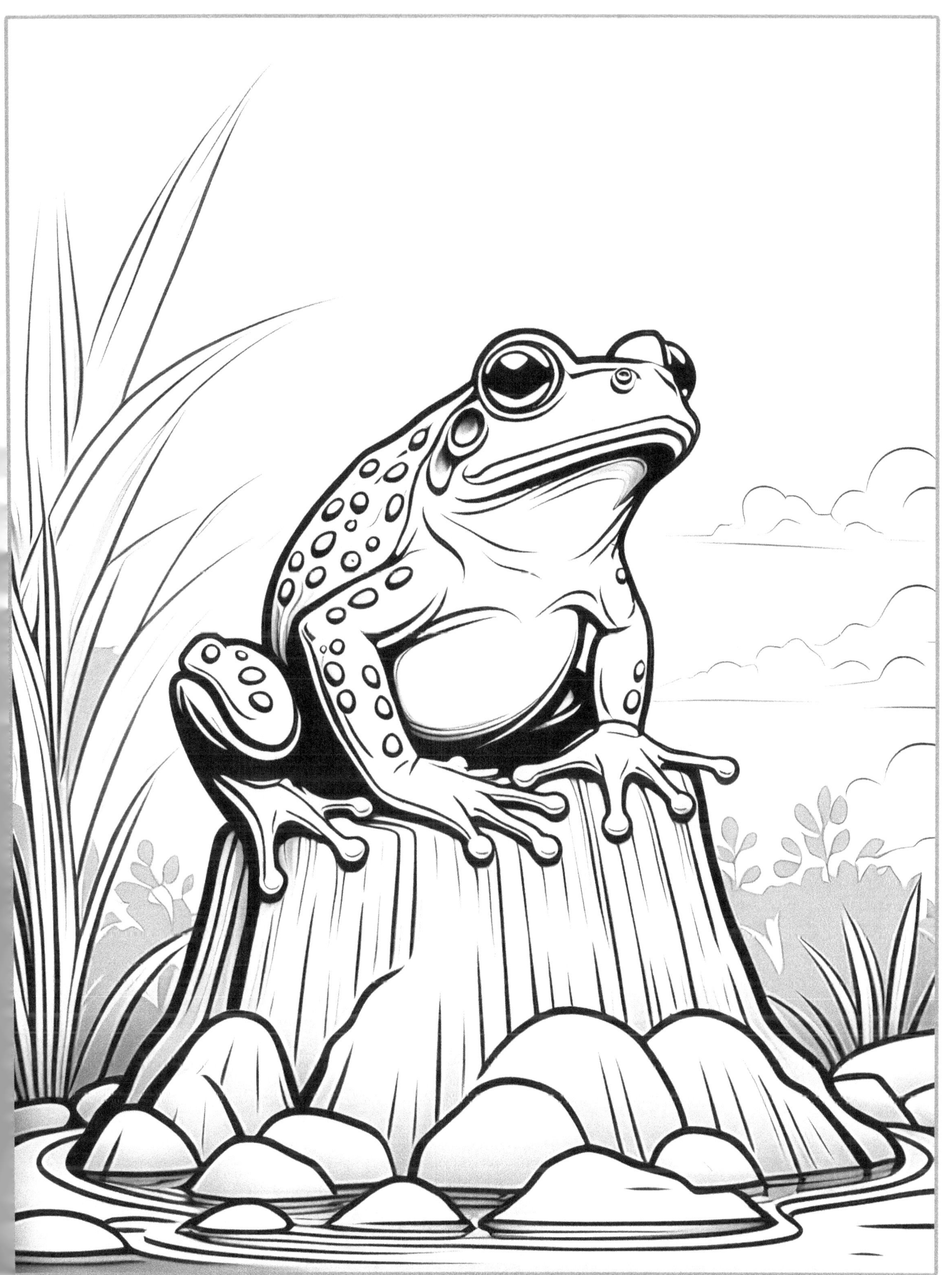

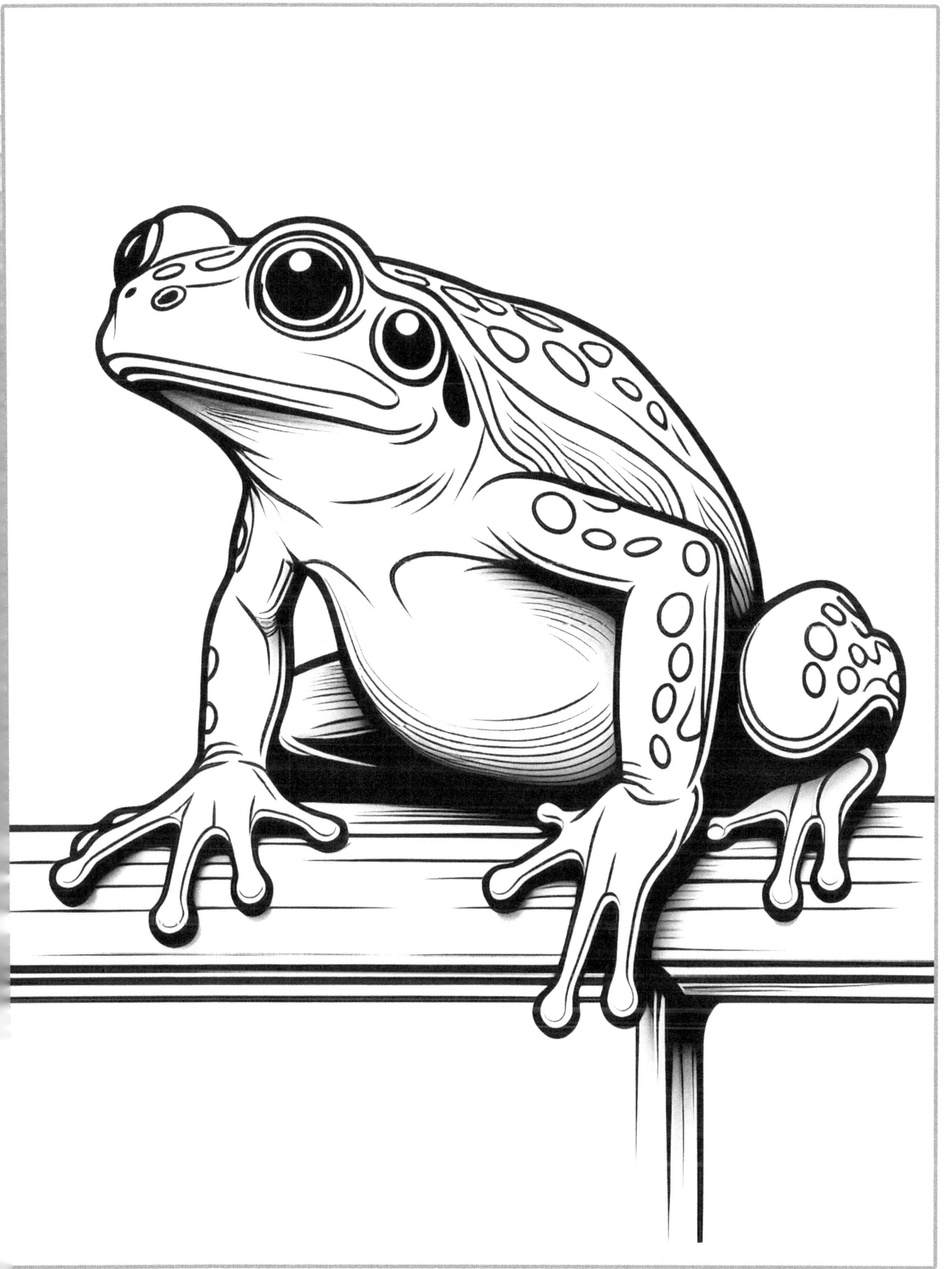

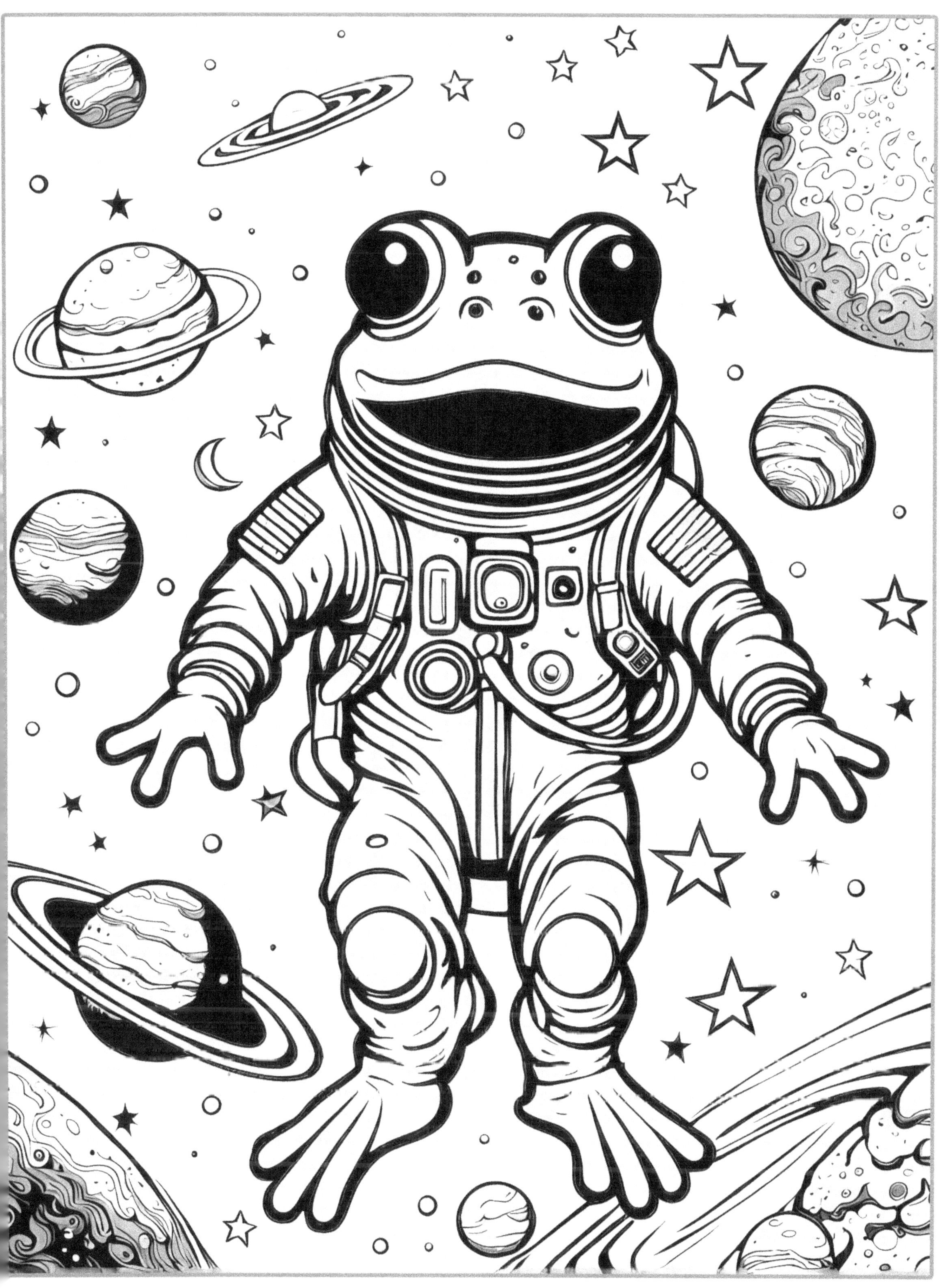

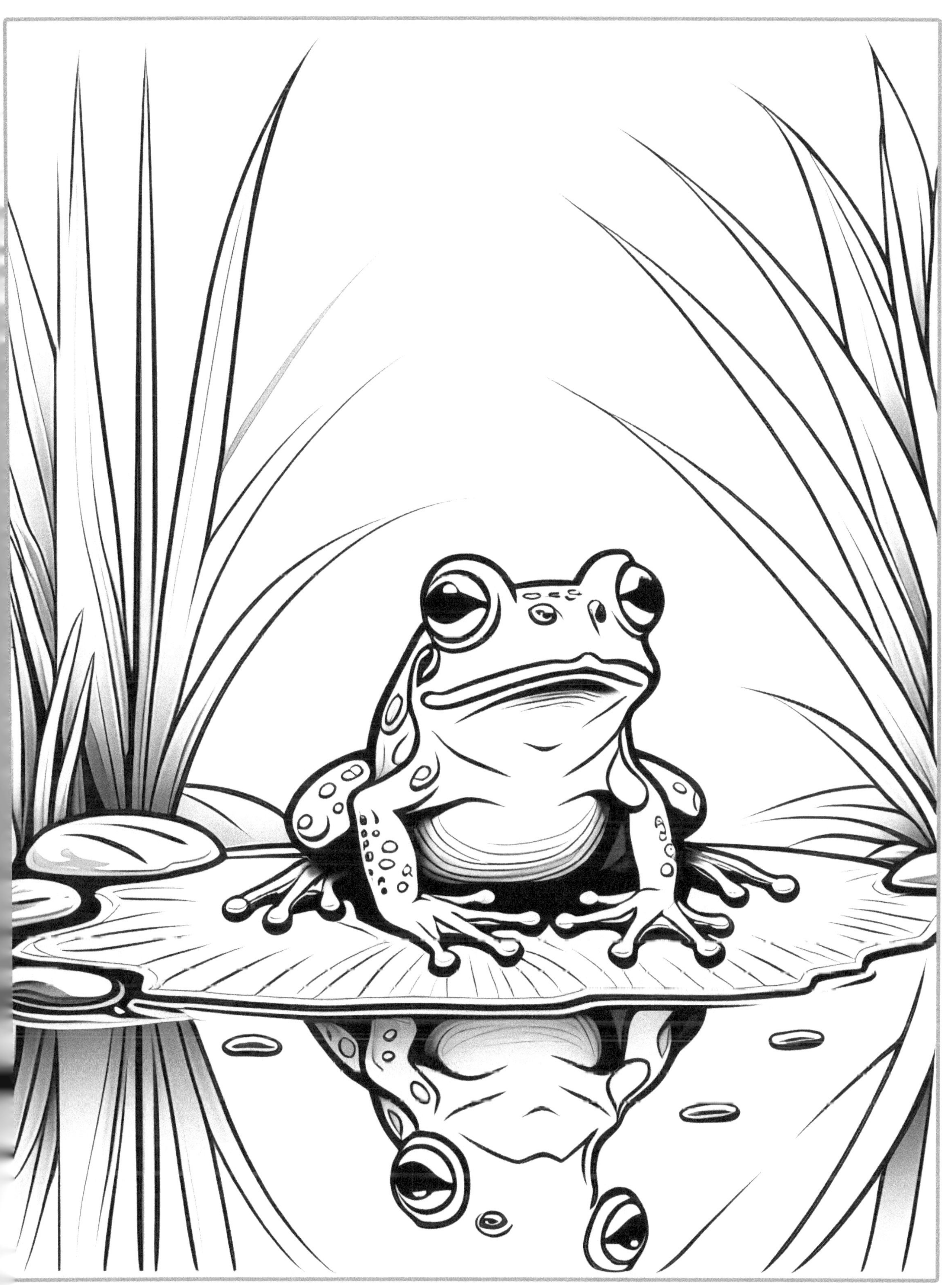

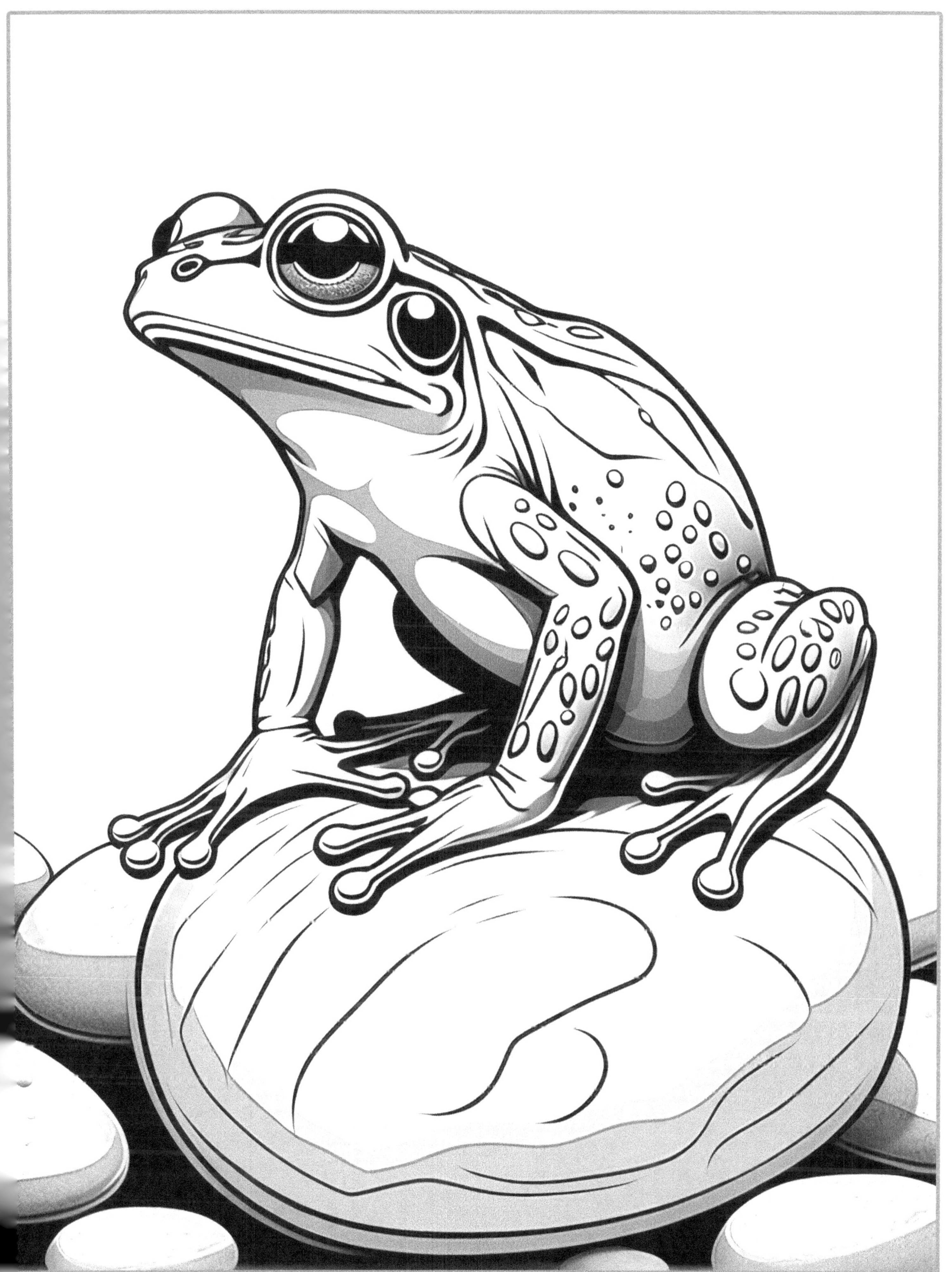

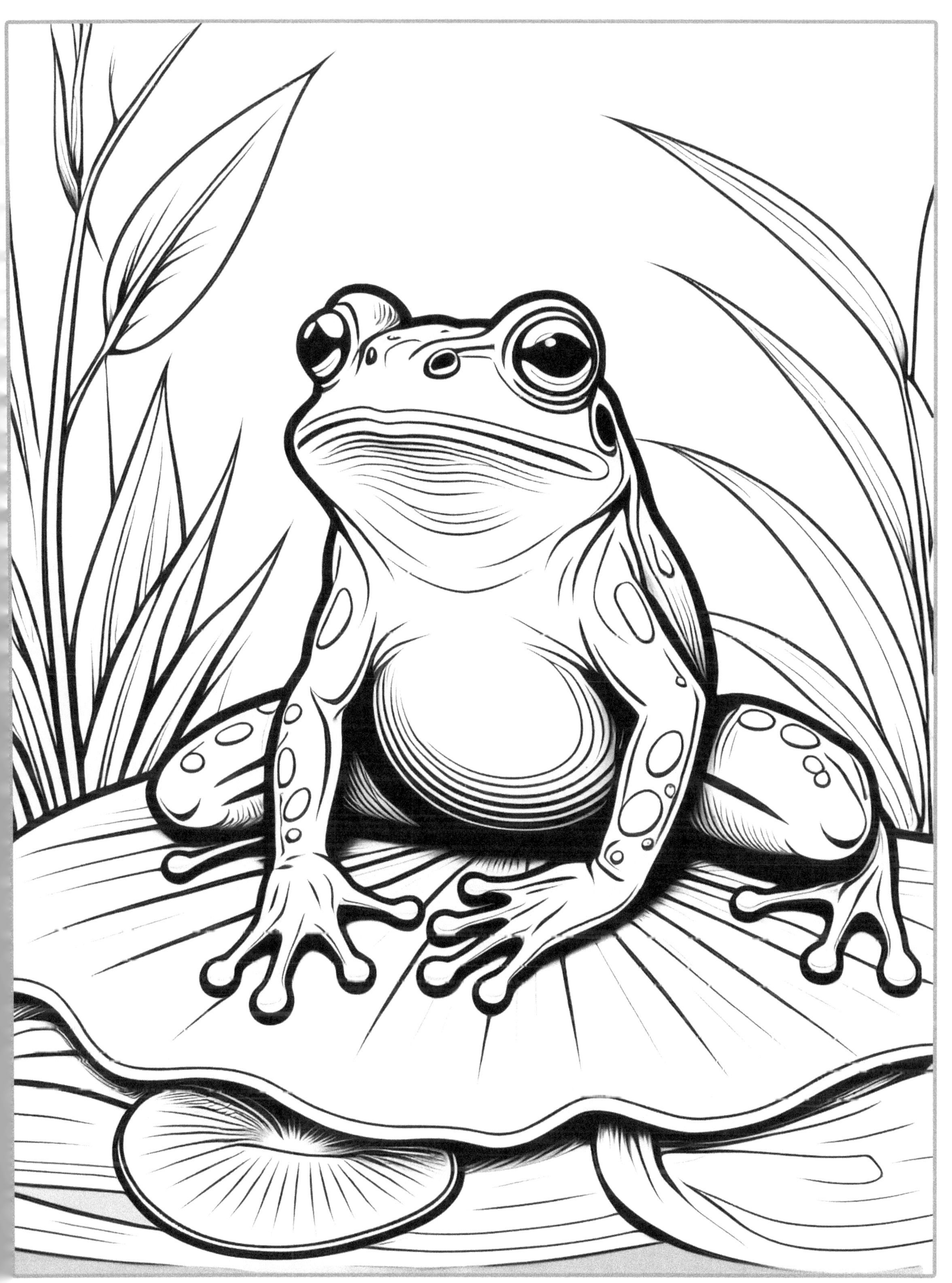

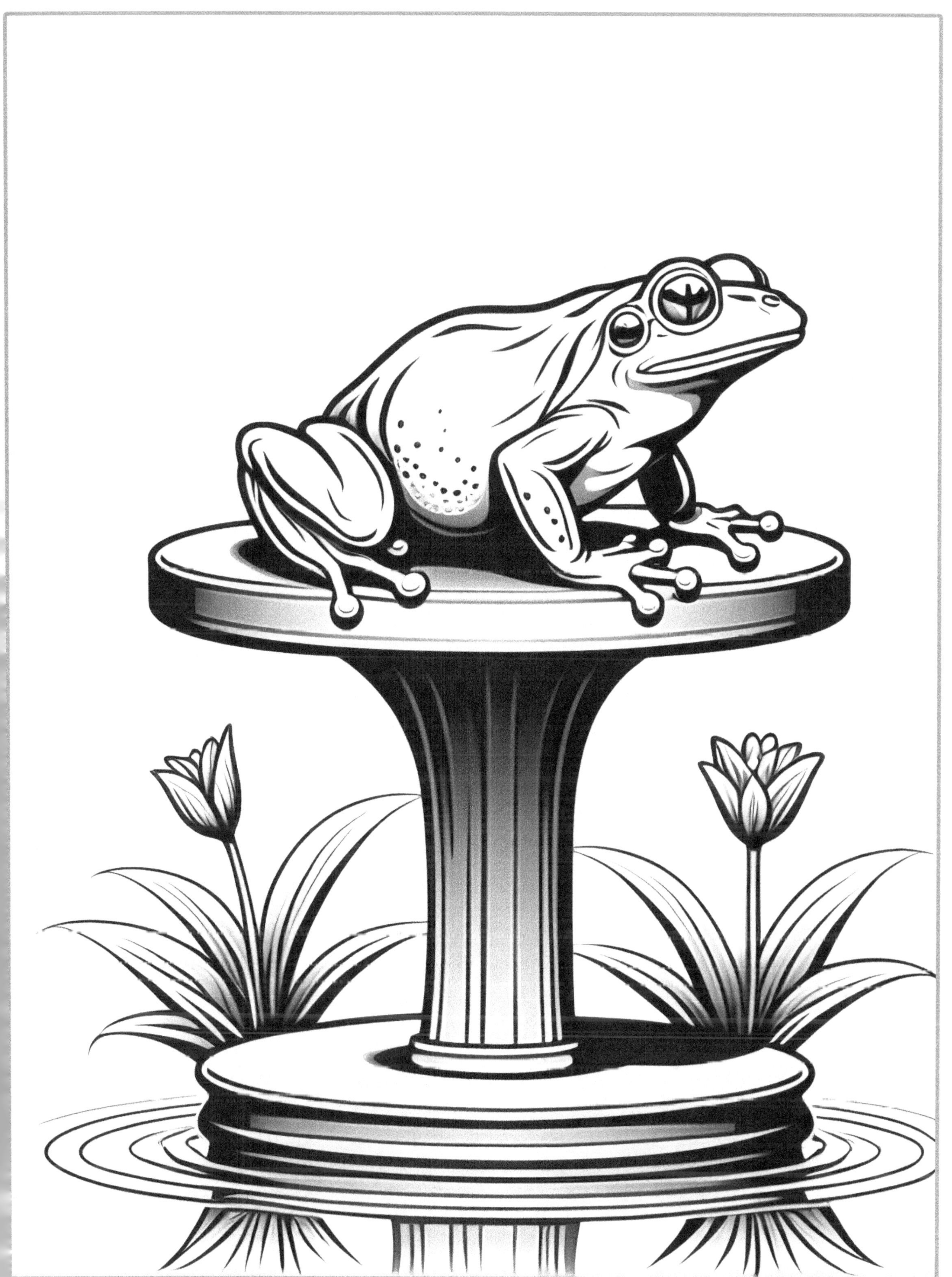

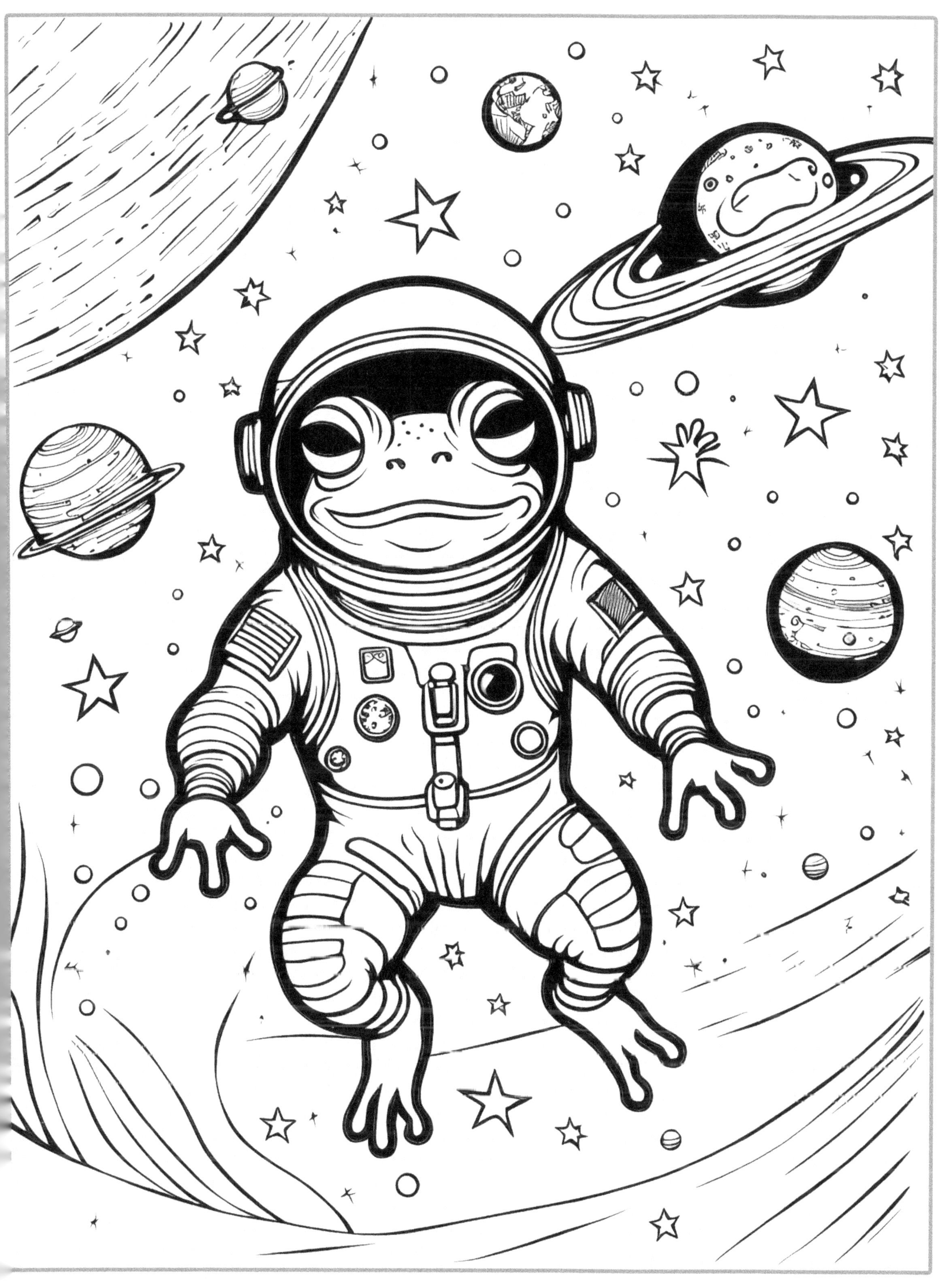

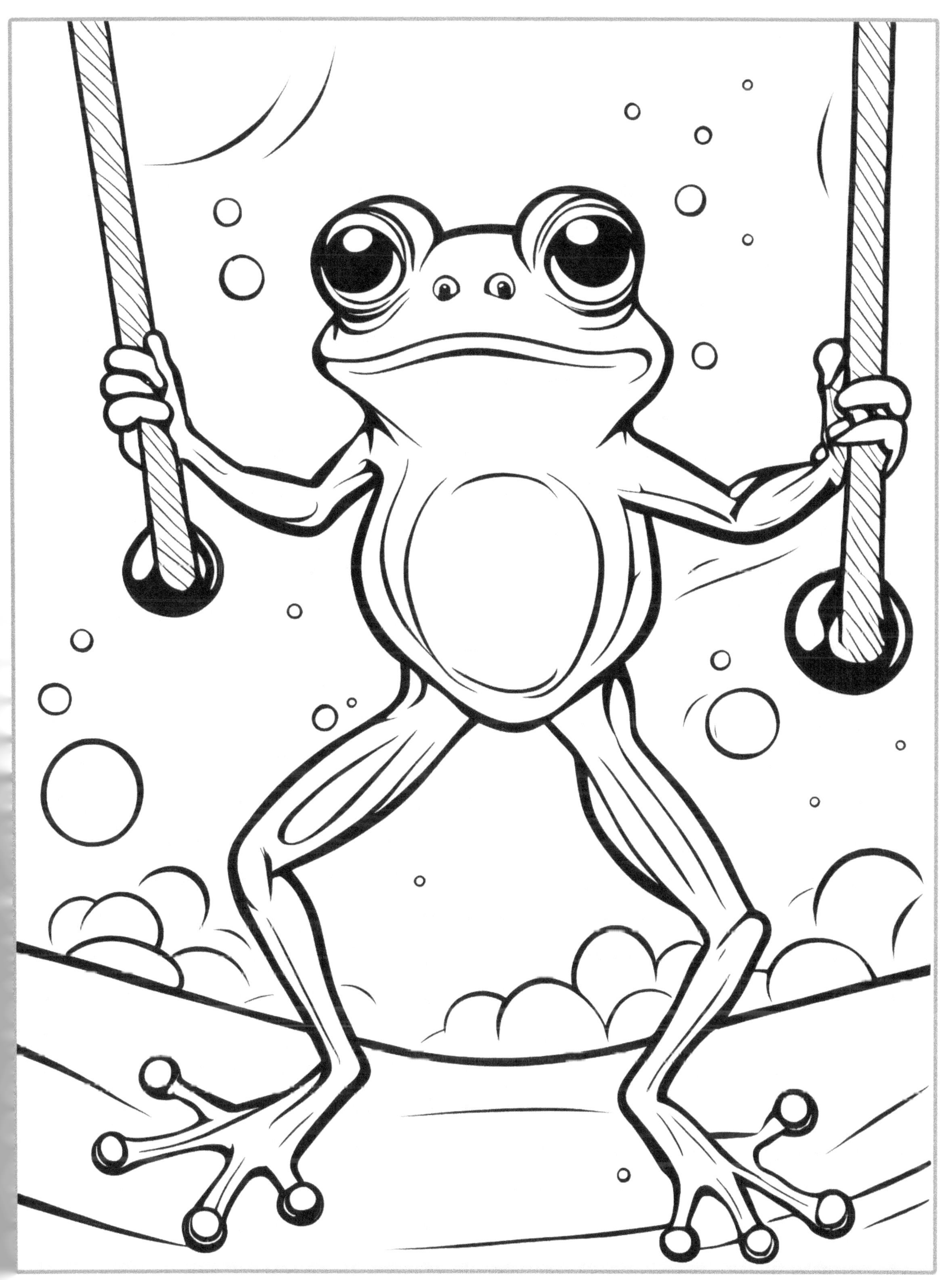

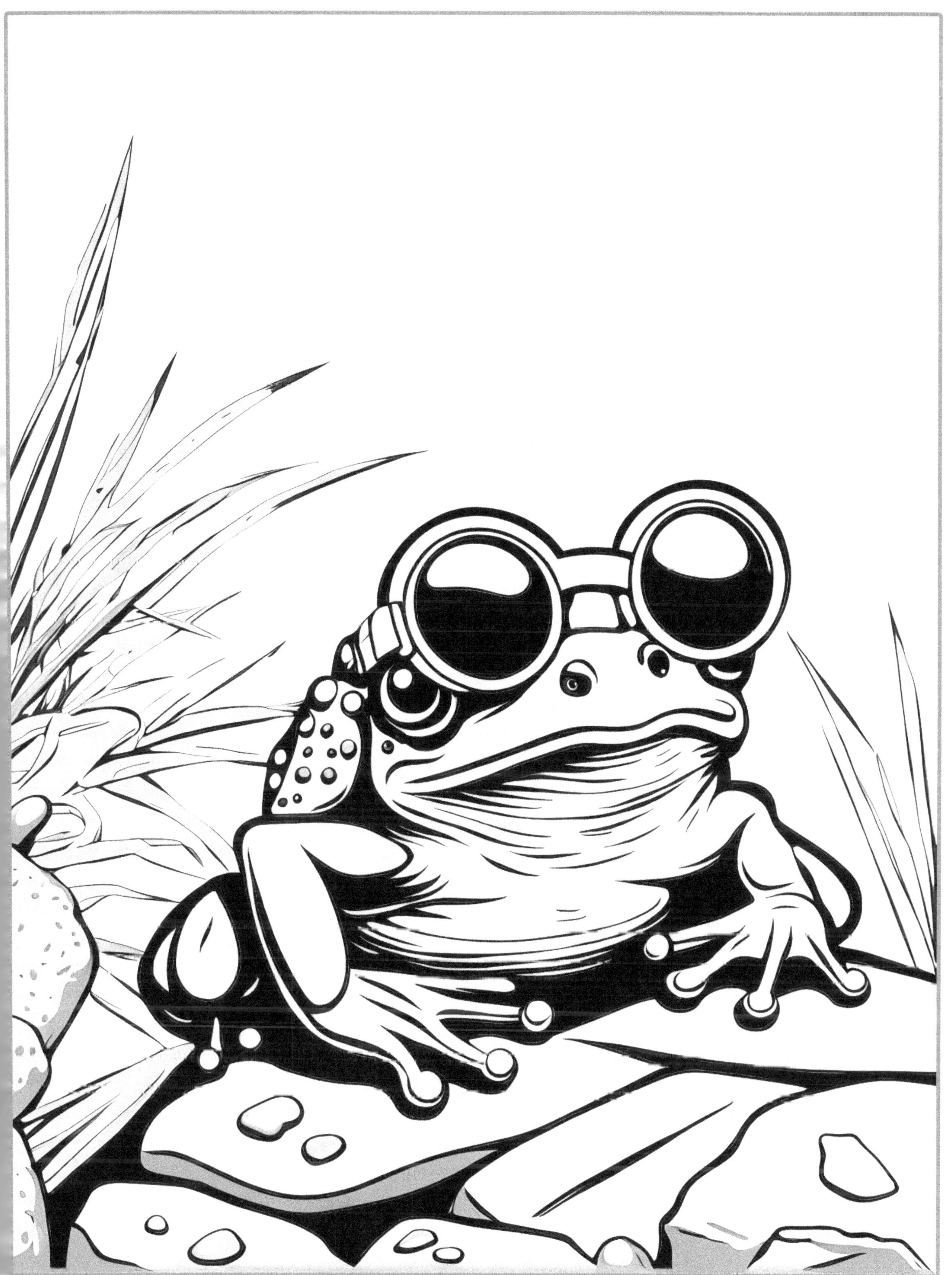